CLASSIC
SPEEDWAY VENUES
PAST & PRESENT

Philip Dalling

HALSGROVE

By the same Author

Speedway titles:

Nottingham and Long Eaton Speedway 1928-1967
The Golden Age of Speedway
Speedway The Classic Era

Local history:

Erewash Valley Portrait

First published in Great Britain in 2013

British Library Cataloguing-in-Publication Data
A CIP record for this title is available from the British Library

ISBN 978 0 85704 212 5

HALSGROVE
Halsgrove House,
Ryelands Business Park,
Bagley Road, Wellington, Somerset TA21 9PZ
Tel: 01823 653777   Fax: 01823 216796
email: sales@halsgrove.com

Part of the Halsgrove group of companies
Information on all Halsgrove titles is available at: www.halsgrove.com

Printed and bound in Great Britain by T.J. International Ltd

CONTENTS

Here's mud in your eye?
Speedway fans over the
decades have become
accustomed to dodging
flying cinders or shale, in
their determination to
get as close to the action
as possible. These
supporters are taking
avoiding action at The
Shay, Halifax, in the days
before stricter health and
safety rules forced
spectators to stand
further back from the
safety fence. (AFC)

ACKNOWLEDGEMENTS

I AM GRATEFUL for the assistance of a great number of people, both within and outside the speedway family, who helped in a variety of ways with the preparation of this volume.

The first group of people to whom acknowledgment is due are the promoters and officials at tracks throughout the country who enabled my visits, provided information and, in some instances, photographs, and who answered my many questions with great patience and courtesy. Thank you to the following: David Gordon, Chris Morton and Richard Frost (Belle Vue), Dennis McCleary (Berwick), Alan Phillips and Chris Simpson (Birmingham Perry Barr), Shona Campbell, David Bellerby, Paul Watson and Kevin Ling (Eastbourne), John Campbell, Mike Hunter and Jim Henry (Edinburgh Armadale), Chris Louis (Ipswich), Tim Allan (Kent), Jonathan Chapman (Kings Lynn), Alan Jones (Leicester Beaumont Park), George English (Newcastle), Rick Frost (Peterborough), Graham Hambly (Plymouth), Giles Hartwell and Steve Allen (Poole), Brian Havelock and Gareth Rogers (Redcar), Debbie Hancock and Ian Belcher (Somerset), Neil Machin (Sheffield), Dave Tattum (Stoke), Gary Patchett, Alun Rossiter and Andy Pavey (Swindon), Laura Morgan and Steve Whitehead (Workington).

The second category of people who afforded me invaluable assistance are those who provided information and photographs from current or defunct tracks. Thanks are due to Guy Allott, Nicky Allott, Bob Andrews, Vic Ashton, Rob Bamford, Geoff Bennett, The British Olympic Association, Brian Bott, Colin Burnett, Ian Bush, John Carpenter, John Chaplin, Peter Colvin, Berris Connoly, Ray Cresp, Steve Dixon, Dudley Archives and Local History Service, Danny Dunton, Lee Dunton, Reg Duval, Reg and Eileen Fearman, Clive Featherby, Hugh Flouch, Derek France, Ove Fundin, Edward Garvey, David Green, Bert Harkins, John Harper and the Tamworth Herald, John Hart, Ian Hitchcock, Richard Hollingsworth, Penny Icke and the Royal Commission on the Ancient and Historical Monuments of Wales, Alan Jay, Stuart Jay and Derek Jay, Michael Kemp, Hilda Lawson, Elaine Whitehead of Long Eaton Public Library, Brian Longman, Tony McDonald of Retro Speedway, Dic Mortimer, Mike Moseley, Brian Owen, Chris O'Connor of Tamworth Library, Ole Olsen and Torben Olsen, Frederick Pallett, Ernest Palmer, Dave Parry, Colin Parker, Colin Poole, Bill Powell, Nicola Sands of IMG, Len Silver, John Skinner of the Defunct Speedway Tracks Website, *Speedway Researcher*, *Speedway Plus*, John Somerville, Francesca Stadelmayr, Alex Summerfield of

Bullet Images, Paul Taylor, The University of East London, Vic White, Sarah Williams of Tamworth Castle Museum, Peter Wrathall. All photographs are individually credited in the text, using the code outlined below.

The continued advice and assistance of Steven Pugsley, Sharon O'Inn and Karen Binaccioni at Halsgrove has been invaluable.

Brenda Dyer has been the perfect companion on my visits to speedway tracks throughout the country, patient at all times and a source of inspiration and encouragement.

Photographic credits code:

A	= Author
AC	= Author's Collection
AFC	= Allott Family Collection
AS	= Alex Summerfield (Bullet Images)
BA	= Bob Andrews
BC	= Berris Connoly
BBC	= Brian Bott Collection
BL	= Brian Longman
BVS/RF	= Belle Vue Speedway/Richard Frost
CB	= Colin Burnett
CMC	= Chris Morton Collection
CP	= Colin Poole
CPC	= Colin Parker
DA	= Dudley Archives and Local History Service
EG	= Edward Garvey
FP	= Frederick Pallett
GB	= Geoff Bennett
HL	= Hilda Lawson
IB	= Ian Bush
IH	= Ian Hitchcock
IMG	= IMG Worldwide
JFC	= Jay Family Collection
JC	= John Carpenter
KH	= Kathy Hitchen
LEPL	= Long Eaton Public Library
MKC	= Mike Kemp Collection
MMC	= Mike Moseley Collection
NMW	= National Museum of Wales
RDC	= Reg Duval Collection
RS	= Retro Speedway
RFC	= Reg Fearman Collection
RH	= Rob Hollingsworth
RN/RSO	= R. Nicholson/R.S. Oliver
SD	= Steve Dixon
TH/JH	= *Tamworth Herald*/John Harper
VA	= Vic Ashton

Note: Every effort has been made to achieve accuracy in the acknowledgment of photographs.

INTRODUCTION

COMPETITIVE SPEEDWAY has been staged at some 200 tracks in the United Kingdom of Great Britain and Northern Ireland.

Add the venues which have staged long-track racing, beach racing, grass-track racing, demonstrations and training sessions, and the number of sites which have reverberated to the roar of speedway and similar machines is virtually doubled.

An amazing variety of venues have staged either league racing or licensed individual meetings, including the great national sporting venues of England, Scotland and Wales, and greyhound tracks of all sizes, from palatial metropolitan arenas down to primitive circuits in the 'flapping track' category.

Speedway has been staged in stadia built for football, both codes of rugby, cycling, athletics and even cricket. The sport has operated on agricultural showgrounds, on a former airfield, and on sites originally used for the trotting variety of horse racing.

Because of the ready availability of greyhound stadia and other established facilities in the years of speedway's mushroom growth, the number of venues which could genuinely claim to have been constructed specifically for speedway was, for many decades, relatively small.

That situation has changed, as the loss of long-established venues, greyhound stadia in particular, has prompted the creation of new facilities for speedway on greenfield (or brownfield) sites. These new venues are either direct replacements for lost stadia, or have served to introduce the sport to districts where it had never previously been staged.

Interest in sporting venues is widespread and increasing. Bookshop shelves are bursting with volumes on the homes, past and present, of football, cricket, motor racing, motor cycle racing, horse racing and golf.

The various homes of speedway have been carefully and exhaustively catalogued in that excellent book, *The Homes of British Speedway,* by Robert Bamford and John Jarvis.

It is a classic of its kind, has long been one of my favourite bedside books, and has been an inspiration for this volume. *Classic Speedway Venues* is not designed to compete with or in any way supersede a work which I wholeheartedly recommend to any speedway fan who has yet to buy and read it.

Instead, when commissioned to produce a work on the subject of speedway venues, I set out to take the reader on the sort of tour of speedway's heartlands that I myself would regard as a heaven-sent opportunity.

It was decided at an early stage to feature the 28 tracks which constituted the membership of British speedway's three leagues – the Elite, Premier and National – at the start of the 2013 season, together with the venue for the British Grand Prix. It was agreed, in consultation with the publisher, that these 29 current venues would be supplemented with an equal number of tracks which, for one reason or another, no longer stage speedway racing.

The need to limit the number of tracks covered overall in the book to 58 was governed not only by space considerations but also by a determination from the outset that each venue described would be appropriately illustrated.

My first thought was that the proposed tour of speedway venues past and present which formed the inspiration for the book would be essentially a virtual journey.

As it turned out, the desire to visit new tracks meant that instead of trawling the internet and ploughing through old magazines and record books, I took to the road.

Over a period of three months I visited all but four of the 29 currently operating speedway venues, covering some 3,000 miles in the process, from Eastbourne to Edinburgh and Poole to Peterborough. The fact that I had over the years managed to visit a roughly equivalent number of tracks that had ceased to stage the sport meant that, in the great majority of cases, I have been able to write about the chosen venues from personal experience.

Although there was an initial inclination to present the venues geographically, it was finally decided to place the featured tracks into categories based primarily on either their status or the purpose for which they were originally constructed. At the same time care has been taken to achieve a good geographical spread.

The primitive facilities at High Beech were quickly improved. This 1930s shot shows the substantial grandstand and extensive banking for spectators on the bends. Various types of motorcycle sport enjoyed a brief boom in the late 1920s and 1930s and on this occasion a High Beech team is taking on a Wembley side at motorcycle polo – a dangerous occupation if the spectacle of a player falling head first out of the sidecar without a crash helmet is any guide. (AC)

Six categories eventually emerged, illustrating respectively the great national stadia where speedway has been staged, the iconic and glamorous London arenas of the sport's golden age, the provincial greyhound stadia which have played a major role in the sport's development, followed by the football grounds, from both the round and oval ball codes.

The fifth category features the perhaps surprisingly large number of circuits built primarily for speedway, while the final section explores a small selection of venues which developed for a variety of purposes, making them unsuitable for slotting in to the earlier well-defined categories.

Inevitably, some featured tracks overlap the categories. The Empire Stadium, Wembley, was at one and the same time a national stadium, a London arena, a football ground and a greyhound stadium. Its status as a great national stadium dictated its place in the first category.

Odsal, Bradford, essentially a rugby league ground, gained inclusion in the national stadia category as the venue for two speedway World Finals.

My intention has been to capture the essential flavour of speedway's venues – their architectural features, their varied levels of spectator facility, and also their social contribution to their individual communities.

Many of the keenest speedway fans will have achieved a tally of venues visited which considerably exceeds my own relatively modest total of 50. On the other hand, a significant number of fans will not have strayed too far from their home track.

I hope they will find this book of considerable interest in opening up broader horizons within the wonderful world of British speedway racing.

Philip Dalling
Exmoor and The Peak District, 2013

*Note: At the time of going to press the possibility of speedway returning to Bradford's Odsal Stadium, and to a new venue at the Showground in the former hotbed of Norwich, was being seriously discussed.

Separated by 85 years of speedway history. Pictured below left is High Beech, Epping Forest, in 1928, with Australian pioneer Billy Galloway taking a tumble behind a club rider on an Ariel machine. Pictured below right is Central Park, Sittingbourne, the home of the sport's newest club, Kent Kings, which raced its first match in May 2013 (AC/A)

The main turnstiles at Belle Vue's Hyde Road Stadium in the venue's latter years, after the stadium had been purchased by Bamforth Leisure. (KH)

The traditional turnstiles at Kings Lynn's Norfolk Arena have been replaced by a box office equipped with state-of-the-art touch screen ticket machines. (A)

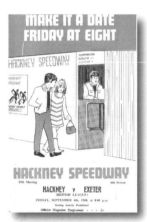

Buying a programme is often the first step after gaining admission to the stadium. At Hackney in the late 1960s promoter Len Silver took his marketing inspiration from the youth culture of the 'swinging sixties'. (AC)

Programmes in the second decade of the 21st century are much glossier than their earlier counterparts, acting as match day magazines as well as racecards. (AC)

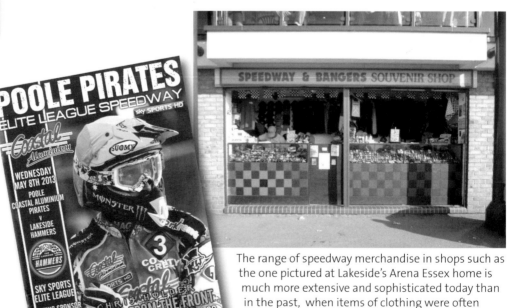

The range of speedway merchandise in shops such as the one pictured at Lakeside's Arena Essex home is much more extensive and sophisticated today than in the past, when items of clothing were often limited to ties for men and headscarves for women, rosettes in the team colours and portrait photographs of the riders. (BL)

Chapter One

THROUGH THE TURNSTILES ...

From the February day in 1928 when the unexpected size of the crowd at the inaugural High Beech meeting overwhelmed the Ilford and District Motor Cycle Club volunteers and their rolls of tickets, countless numbers of spectators, from the committed to the merely curious, have passed through the turnstiles at speedway venues.

The Speedway Control Board recorded in 1949 a record aggregate attendance for the sport of more than 11 million people. In the late 1960s and 1970s, a second golden age, the aggregate attendance for speedway in Britain was generally agreed to be around three and a half million.

Before the introduction of VAT and generally tighter financial reporting procedures, promoters routinely inflated attendance figures in order to make the public believe they were missing out on something worthwhile.

Today, managements are still coy about official figures, and the speedway media, generally denied exact figures or even rounded-up estimates, commonly resorts to phrases such as 'a bumper' attendance or 'a larger than average crowd', in an effort to fill the gap.

Crowds obviously do matter, and not just in terms of being sufficient to guarantee a track's financial health. For the riders, being cheered on a parade by several thousand spectators has to be more satisfying than riding past the empty void that is now commonplace, with spectators confined to small areas of a stadium or spread so thinly that it hardly makes a difference.

Despite smaller crowds and consequent lack of atmosphere, the commitment of the core fans has not diminished and neither have the routines and rituals of a speedway meeting changed all that much.

Entrance to venues is still achieved by pressing through a turnstile or, on occasions, simply being handed a ticket at a temporary paybox (shades of High Beech in 1928). An exception is the high-tech ticketing system at Kings Lynn (see pages 10 and 101).

Buying a programme, picking up a magazine or team merchandise at the track shop or stall, having a look at the machines warming up in the pits (at those tracks where the

Pie and peas at the South Tees Motor Park in Redcar can be washed down with a pint in the clubhouse, which has its own traditional inn sign. (A)

The appetite of fans for snacks before, during and after the match is one aspect of a night at speedway which has hardly changed. Rye House has a particular reputation for the quality of its food, and service comes with a smile. (IB)

riders are still visible) is all part of the process of a weekly visit to speedway.

Fans have favourite viewing positions, congregating with their friends at the same spot every week to exchange news and views and have a moan about the sport's rule-makers. All this has barely changed in decades.

The inner man (and woman) has never been neglected at speedway meetings. From the start the original greyhound stadia had facilities far in advance of those at football and other grounds, and it has long been possible for speedway fans to enjoy a three course meal served at your table in a glass-fronted grandstand.

If your taste is for something less formal (and less pricey), the inevitable hot dog stands and mobile bars are an alternative.

Many fans like to arrive early at a track to get a good position close to the pits. Kings Lynn's pit area is sited close to the first bend, and the activities of the riders and mechanics can be viewed throughout the meeting, particularly from the first turn terracing. (A)

Having taken your favourite spot in a traditional grandstand, in a glass-fronted bar or restaurant, on the terraces (covered if you are lucky), or simply on a wide-open grass or cinder bank, the next vital step in a speedway meeting is a proper parade.

Some tracks stick to the traditional method of lining up the machines on either side of the start line, with either the announcer or the centre green presenter introducing the riders individually, starting with the visitors and building up to the home favourites.

A combination of present-day health and safety demands and the modern trend of extensive practice starts and laps means the riders are usually fairly anonymous in their face-covering helmets. An acceptable alternative is to parade the riders around the circuit on a towed trailer, which at least allows the fans to get a proper view of the contestants.

The formal announcer, whose job it is to make sure the spectators receive quick and accurate information about heat results and times, vital if programmes are to be correctly completed, has for many seasons now played second fiddle to the meeting presenter.

Spotting speedway's celebrities, like Chris Louis (pictured centre), twice British Champion and now Ipswich director of speedway and Witches team manager, is a favourite pastime. (A)

Autograph hunting seems to have lost some of its appeal for modern supporters. Back in the fifties the Norwich Stars' top man and World Champion, Swedish ace Ove Fundin, leans over the pits barrier to sign for some young fans. (RFC)

It looks like decision time for a pensive Alun Rossiter, former rider and now co-promoter and team manager with his hometown club, Swindon Robins. On the evening in question Rossiter's men won vital away points at Peterborough's East of England Showground. (A)

Left: When it is time to choose a favourite viewing spot for the meeting, fans usually have a variety of options. Early arrivals at Foxhall Heath, Ipswich, take their customary seats in the small traditional grandstand by the start line, with its bench seats. (A)

At many stadiums today, particularly those which are primarily greyhound tracks, the best view for fans is from the covered bars and restaurants. Purists still prefer to watch without a layer of plate glass between themselves and the action. This is the view from the stand at Newcastle. (A)

Standing terraces, sometimes covered, more often open, still exist at many circuits, particularly on the bends. Supporters at Eastbourne's Arlington Stadium have a good view from the first and second turns across to the home straight, which features an extensive covered terrace, and the start line, dominated by the venue's distinctive race control tower. (A)

The Rebels' flag billows out at the top of the grass banking on the windy Somerset Levels. Despite the rural location of the Oak Tree Arena, the busy M5 Motorway is only the width of a field away behind the supporters. (A)

Not all speedway fans can manage the steps of grandstands or terraces. Rye House is one track where good provision is made for those supporters with disabilities. The area pictured has ample space for wheelchairs and adjacent seats for carers. (IB)

Colourful mascots are an integral part of the modern speedway scene. These Plymouth supporters at Somerset's Oak Tree Arena on a cool spring evening are staying close for warmth to their own Red Devil! (A)

Above right: Edinburgh's mascot is truly the Monarch of all he surveys at Armadale Stadium. (A)

They did things differently in the past. Martin Morley (left), Newcastle mascot and the son of the then Diamonds' team manager, Maurice Morley, admires the miniature machine ridden by his Sheffield counterpart, Nicky Allott, son of Tigers' skipper Guy Allott. The picture was taken at Sheffield's Owlerton Stadium in the early 1960s. Nicky, and later his son Adam, also rode for the Tigers, following in the footsteps of their father and grandfather and of Guy's brother Tommy. (AFC)

The track walk by riders and officials from both sides is now a customary pre-meeting ritual. Somerset's Oak Tree Arena track near Highbridge and Burnham on Sea is the scene of this particular inspection of the circuit. (A)

The relationship between fans and riders has traditionally been a warm one in speedway, and supporters have always helped to raise cash for new equipment and for injured team men. Pictured above are Hackney star Zenon Plech and the track's long-serving supporters' club secretary, Snowy Beattie. (AC)

Despite the hectic lifestyle of many riders today, racing for clubs in the UK, Poland and Sweden, the rapport with the fans remains largely intact. Seven times British Champion Scott Nicholls, well wrapped up against the cold of a May evening in the pits at Eastbourne's Arlington Stadium, chats to supporters of his current club, Coventry, before the start of the meeting. (A)

Someone has to do it! Marking out the white line on the inside of the track, pictured here underway at Workington's Derwent Park home, is a necessary pre-meeting chore. (A)

Without the referee, there can be no racing. FIM official Christina Turnbull prepares for the forthcoming meeting in the well-appointed race control centre at Workington. (A)

Many presenters are excellent, and add to the enjoyment of the meeting. Others should, if the venue is shared with greyhound racing, be confined to one of the kennels until the meeting is over.

The immense pressure of riding speedway at the top level, and in some cases in three different countries in a week, means that one once-common after meeting feature, the get-together in the bar allowing riders to mix with fans, is now relatively rare.

The referee's decision may be binding, but it is not always popular with a rider excluded for some offence. Bo Petersen of Hackney is pictured making his way up the steps to the referee's box to make his point in person – an activity much discouraged by officialdom. (AC)

Whatever the case, and often whatever the result (provided the racing itself has been enjoyable), a night or an afternoon at the speedway means a couple of hours away from life's duller routines. A brief and usually satisfying glimpse of speedway heaven. Long may the experience continue to be available for us all to enjoy.

However stimulating the pre-match rituals may be, the fans are essentially there to watch the racing. A packed grandstand at Leicester's former Blackbird Road home watches a 1951 National League Division Two clash between the local Hunters and visiting Motherwell. Johnny Carpenter leads from team-mate Harwood Pike, and Eagles Bob Lindsay and Joe Crowther (in white). (JC)

Some sixty years later the grandstand is also full at Rye House, and a re-born Leicester are the visitors. (IB)

With draws a relatively rare phenomenon in speedway, there is usually a winning team. The Hackney side take a once traditional tractor ride, now banned on safety grounds. The visible riders are, from the front, Colin Pratt, Roy Trigg, Brian Davies and John Poyser. (AC)

Chapter Two
NATIONAL STADIA
– the Stately Homes of Speedway

Wembley The Empire Stadium

Cardiff The Millennium Stadium

Glasgow Hampden Park

London Crystal Palace

Bradford Odsal Stadium

Belle Vue Hyde Road

London White City Stadium

SPEEDWAY'S STATELY HOMES, the sport's largest and most glamorous venues, have over the decades comprised only a very select group of stadia.

For many years the accolade of speedway's jewel in the crown was shared between two iconic venues which, sadly, no longer exist.

The old Empire Stadium, Wembley, was home to the fashionable, successful and for long fabulously well-supported Wembley Lions National League Division One speedway team.

It was also the venue on 24 occasions for the World Championship Final, in the days before the creation of the Grand Prix system, and the setting for innumerable test matches and national and international championships and tournaments.

Wembley Stadium, the spiritual home of both the famous Wembley Lions team and the World Speedway Championship, pictured in its later form, roofed all round to stage the 1966 Football World Cup. (MKC)

Belle Vue's Hyde Road Stadium may have been smaller and less grandiose than Wembley, but it more than held its own with its southern rival when it came to history, atmosphere and, arguably, the sheer quality of the racing. Largely, if not entirely, built for speedway, with no greyhound track to act as an extra barrier between the spectators and the action, Hyde Road was a spectacular setting for the exploits of the world's most famous and long-lived team.

Wembley was metropolitan and sophisticated, with a royal box (and occasionally even a royal visitor to a speedway meeting), a swish restaurant, and a reputation for insisting on the highest possible standards.

Belle Vue claimed to be the kiss-me-quick showground of the world, not just of the north of England. The fans who packed its stands and terraces for major annual events

Bradford's Odsal Stadium is the only other British venue to have staged a one-off World Final (on two occasions). In July 1947 the vast West Yorkshire bowl held a crowd reported to be in excess of 47,000 to see England defeat Australia 65-43 in an official Test Match. The Australian team is pictured in front of the packed terraces with Odsal manager and Aussie team manager Johnnie Hoskins. The riders, left to right, are Aub Lawson, Max Grosskreutz, Bill Longley, Johnnie Hoskins (manager), Lionel van Praag, Frank Dolan, Ray Duggan, Vic Duggan, Doug McLachlan. (AC)

such as the British League Riders Championship final will never forget its unique atmosphere.

Scotland's national football stadium, Hampden Park, staged speedway racing for just four seasons. The sheer audacity displayed by the Glasgow Tigers promoters in clinching a deal to stage the sport in an arena which at the time speedway moved in was still capable of holding more than 135,000 spectators, gives Hampden (now, like Wembley, redeveloped and unrecognisable) the right to claim a place among speedway's elite venues.

The old Wembley was truly a one-off. Yet the staging of major sporting events of both national and international importance places two other London venues, Crystal Palace and the White City Stadium, in the category of speedway's stately homes.

Sadly, Crystal Palace, which in 1913 held more than 120,000 spectators when Aston Villa beat Sunderland 1-0 in the FA Cup Final, and the White City Stadium, built for the 1908 London Olympics and with a nominal six figure capacity, staged speedway only for relatively brief periods of time.

As a truly major venue, Belle Vue had only one rival in the north of England. Odsal Stadium, Bradford stakes a legitimate claim for inclusion as a stately home for two reasons, as the largest sports arena outside London and the only UK venue outside Wembley to host World Championship Finals.

All of the stadia described to date in this chapter belong essentially to the past as far as speedway is concerned. Both Wembley and Hampden Park are entirely new stadia, although built on the same site, and in the case of Wembley the Football Association, which had much to do with speedway being evicted from the old stadium, has ensured that the sport is purposely and firmly excluded from the new.

White City disappeared under the weight of a BBC television centre (ironic in view of that organisation's refusal to acknowledge speedway today). The Crystal Palace site is now home to an athletics stadium.

Belle Vue's Hyde Road was a victim at least in part of the demand for better safety at sports grounds in the aftermath of the Hillsborough disaster and the Valley Parade, Bradford fire. Odsal, despite the construction of new hospitality facilities at the pits end, could from a physical point of view stage speedway again in the future, and may well do so.

Belle Vue Aces survived the demise of Hyde Road to return to speedway's original home in the Gorton district of Manchester, at Kirkmanshulme Lane. The proposal to construct a new stadium on a site next to the greyhound track, to be known as the National Speedway Stadium, staging major national and international meetings as well as providing a home for the Aces, may soon add a new contender for the status of a stately home for the sport.

The 21st century's stately home is the magnificent Millennium Stadium at Cardiff which, at the time of writing, has staged 13 British Speedway Grand Prix events, annually achieving the modern miracle of seeing a track laid for a one-off meeting.

The British round of the Grand Prix system which has replaced the old World Championship format transforms the streets around Cardiff's Millennium Stadium into an official Fanzone before the meeting, with stalls and entertainment. Many of the fans in this 2012 shot are wearing T-shirts in memory of Lakeside star Lee Richardson, killed in a track crash in Poland earlier in that season. (IMG)

Wembley The Empire Stadium

Speedway racing and Wembley's Empire Stadium were, for a long time, believed to be mutually dependent.

Designed as the centrepiece of the British Empire Exhibition, the stadium was originally destined to be simply a temporary facility, to be demolished once the exhibition closed.

Wembley's promoters doubted the stadium would be viable as a stand-alone sporting venue. Their forebodings would have been justified had it not been for the vision of entrepreneur Arthur Elvin.

The stadium, as predicted, went into liquidation after the Exhibition, but a series of complicated financial manoeuvres saw it come under Elvin's control. Once installed as chairman of the company that now owned the stadium, Elvin had to make the venue pay, in the days when cup finals and international football matches were few in number, and pop concerts and other events unknown.

His answer was to introduce first greyhound racing, providing a year-round income, and then speedway. Without the input of the two now highly unfashionable and scorned sports, Wembley would undoubtedly have been closed and demolished.

England's sporting history would have been very different…

For decades Wembley needed greyhound racing and speedway to flourish. Equally, from 1929 until 1956, it was more or less taken for granted that speedway's economic health and its credibility depended upon its continuance at the Empire Stadium.

The fans gather at the old Wembley, with the stadium in its speedway mode and the greyhound track covered in sheeting to catch flying shale. Note the none-too-comfortable bench seats along the lower tiers of the stadium, and the standing terraces (later banned from top-level football stadia), with crush barriers as a not always completely effective means of stopping crowds swaying towards the front of the enclosures. (MKC)

A highly atmospheric shot at the Empire Stadium, showing the view of the home straight and the starting area from the pits. (MKC)

Wembley was not immune however from speedway's mid-1950s dip in popularity, and the huge post-war crowds at the Empire Stadium suffered a sharp decline. Elvin, a great champion of the sport, kept the Lions alive but when he died prematurely in early 1957, his fellow directors seized the opportunity to withdraw from league racing.

Although some speedway journalists at the time of the 1957 demise of the Wembley Lions predicted that the apocalypse had arrived for the sport, there was at least the silver lining that the Empire Stadium would continue to be available for the World Final and other major meetings.

Although Wembley eventually lost its position as the sole venue used for the World Final, it still managed to dominate the event during the 1960s, staging six out of that decade's ten finals.

The 1970s opened brightly with the revival of the Wembley Lions team in 1970, but the pressure from other sports, particularly from the traditionally anti-speedway Football Association, brought an end to league racing at the end of the second season.

Wembley staged three World Finals during the rest of the decade, together with other international speedway events, but the writing was on the wall, and the 1981 World Final saw the sport's swansong at the Empire Stadium.

With the planned sale of the stadium to the Football Association for complete demolition and reconstruction, the dogs also eventually outstayed their welcome, with the final greyhound meeting held just before Christmas 1998.

Subsequent venues for the one-off World Finals in Britain (Odsal) and elsewhere in the world generally failed to provide an attendance anywhere near the figure of 92,000 achieved for the last Wembley final in 1981.

Big meetings need the glamour of an iconic national stadium. The proof lies in the fact that despite the declining level of interest in speedway in the UK, the British event at Cardiff's superb Millennium Stadium attracts by far the largest crowd for a Speedway Grand Prix, under the modern World Championship system.

Following the demise of the Lions after the 1956 season, Wembley continued to host not just the World Final and other important individual meetings but also test matches. Pictured is the Great Britain team which defeated Soviet Russia in July 1964. Pictured, l-r, are: Barry Briggs, Mike Broadbank, Ron How, Ken McKinlay, Nigel Boocock, Brian Brett, Ray Cresp and Leo McAuliffe. The terraces behind the riders are not as well populated as in past years, with an official attendance for the meeting of 26,800. (AC)

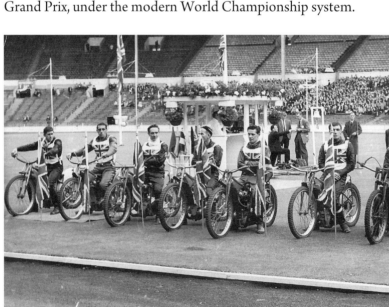

The old Wembley, even after it was refurbished for the 1966 Football World Cup, could be uncomfortable, with backless wooden benches the rule in many seated parts of the stadium. When it was decided to transform the arena into an all-seater stadium, equally uncomfortable plastic seats with no backrests were simply bolted on to the terraces.

It says much for the appeal of Wembley that fans, intoxicated by the sheer atmosphere of the venue on World Final night and the decades of speedway history which the stadium reflected, were prepared to ignore the rapidly dating and often shabby facilities.

The Empire Stadium is still sadly missed by the generations that knew it in its pomp, and it will never be adequately replaced as a speedway theatre of dreams.

Bradford Odsal Stadium

Glamour is not perhaps the first word that springs to mind when considering Bradford's Odsal Stadium.

As the only UK venue apart from Wembley to stage one-off, sudden-death World Speedway Championship Finals, the arena has an automatic right to inclusion among the stately homes of British speedway.

Odsal's sheer size, which in 2013 still has the ability to take the breath away from the first-time visitor, marks it out from the general run of speedway circuits. Yet even after much costly investment over the years, the arena still gives the impression of being only partly developed.

Its overwhelming size, and the lack, still apparent today, of adequate cover and seating for the majority of patrons, has contributed to its reputation as a controversial venue.

An aerial shot of the huge bowl of Odsal Stadium, Bradford, taken when the venue staged the 1985 one-off World Final, in front of a crowd of around 35,000 people. A second World Final was staged at Odsal in 1990. (AC)

Odsal in the late 1940s, with a huge crowd overflowing from the concrete terracing on to the steep cinder and grass banks at the top of the bowl. (AC)

The site was formerly a rubbish tip, and in 1933 140,000 cart loads of household waste had to be cleared away before a rugby pitch could be laid, with a 2,000-seat grandstand and acres of bare clinker banking. The stadium's potential, fully realised after World War Two, became apparent in the pre-war era, with an attendance for a rugby league match of just below 65,000 in 1939.

Bradford Northern RLFC's Harry Hornby's plans for introducing speedway to Odsal were thwarted by the war. When it came to an end he wasted no time in reviving his ambitions, recruiting Johnnie Hoskins (who had failed to gain the post-war promoting rights at West Ham) to inject the speedway know-how required.

After a short season of challenge matches in 1945, Bradford entered the first post-war National League, and the Boomerangs as the side was initially known won the first post-war league match to be staged, at Wimbledon in April 1946.

Odsal reportedly had an average crowd in 1946 of 31,000, and in July 1947 more than 47,000 watched an England-Australia test match. Although speedway was a financial success, there were early problems with the track.

Riders demanded that its initial squarish shape should be changed after a death and several serious injuries and they were backed up by a threat from the Control Board to withdraw the licence if action were not taken.

The stadium's ability to cope with a really big crowd, whatever the state of the spectator accommodation, was tested to the full in May 1954, when the official attendance for a Rugby League Challenge Cup Final replay, featuring Halifax against Warrington, was declared at 102,569 – a record for an English sporting fixture outside Wembley.

Falling crowds as the 1950s and 1960s progressed affected both speedway and rugby league. The track management intended to run open licence speedway in 1957, but the early demise that season of Birmingham brought Odsal back into the by now single division National League. It was only a temporary reprieve, as full closure occurred at the end of the season.

The various revivals at Bradford, as the Panthers in the early 1960s (with the 1962 season being raced at the much smaller Greenhill Autodrome in the city), Bradford

A refurbished Odsal today, still the home of the Bradford Bulls Rugby League team. The grandstand has new seating and there is a hospitality complex on what was the pits bend. The terracing on the first and second bends remains. There is always hope that speedway will return to Odsal. (A)

Northern between 1970 and 1973, the Barons from 1974-76 and finally the Dukes from 1986 to 1997, played to much smaller audiences.

Once Wembley became unavailable, Odsal enjoyed a new lease of life as a venue for major speedway events, staging two World Finals in 1985 and 1990, the 1989 Speedway World Team Cup Final, which Great Britain dominated, and the 1997 British Speedway Grand Prix.

Rugby league's existence over the years has been chequered, and although the Bradford Bulls (a new name for the new era in the sport) set up an attendance record for the RL Superleague in 1999, with more than 24,000 people watching a match against Leeds, crowds in recent years have been much lower and the rugby club has endured a financial crisis.

It is an ill wind that blows nobody any good and the struggles of the rugby club gives hope for the return of speedway. Although a corporate facility has been built at the pits end of the stadium, very close to the disused track, this should not prevent a speedway revival.

What sort of atmosphere speedway would provide in a stadium which even under present-day health and safety regulations has a capacity of 24,000, is difficult to judge.

Odsal's sheer size, perhaps its greatest claim to fame, is also in many ways its Achilles heel.

Cardiff The Millennium Stadium

What a venue the Millennium Stadium would make for an old-style, one-off, sudden-death World Final.

The modern arena has many advantages over the old Empire Stadium (and quite a few, one suspects, over the new version of Wembley).

It provides comfortable seating and good facilities, offers a fine view from every part of the stadium, and its roof guarantees immunity from bad weather.

Cardiff's magnificent Millennium Stadium, on the banks of the River Taff in the heart of the capital city of Wales. (A)

The Millennium's location on the banks of the River Taff in the very heart of Wales' capital city provides a much more attractive location for the milling crowds than was (and is) the case in bleak North London.

The carnival atmosphere in the streets around the stadium is a fine advertisement for speedway. With 13 grands prix to its credit, Cardiff is an established fixture on the

More than 40,000 speedway fans, comprising the largest crowd for any Grand Prix, create an electric atmosphere inside the Millennium Stadium, where a speedway circuit is laid down for just one meeting a year. (IMG)

sport's calendar, and one which is warmly welcomed by the Principality and the city.

Many older speedway fans, given the choice, would opt for a return to the old structure of the World Championship. The qualifying rounds allowed almost any rider holding down a place in a league team to take part in the competition, and it is part of the sport's folklore that Jack Young of Edinburgh won his first title as a rider from the UK's second tier.

The grand prix system, in both theory and practice, allows a rider to accumulate enough points to be declared World Champion without ever winning an individual grand prix. It is only when a certain set of circumstances applies that the title is decided at the last gasp, at the final grand prix.

When this is the case, the tension admittedly can more than match that experienced in a sudden-death final.

Former World Champions in a different form of action at the Cardiff Grand Prix. The creator of the series, Ole Olsen (left) and Barry Briggs make the draw for Britain's biggest meeting of the season, with some attractive assistance. (IMG)

The British Grand Prix, although recent years has seen the date switched around to a certain degree, is not the final and ultimate meeting of the campaign. Given the Millennium Stadium's commitments for rugby and football in the spring and autumn, it is not likely to have that status any time soon, despite the fact that it attracts by some way the biggest crowd of the whole series.

Just imagine the atmosphere in Cardiff if, instead of being simply a contributing factor to the winning of the World title over the long haul, it provided the occasion when the championship was finally decided?

My personal view of the big night at the Millennium Stadium is that it is an occasion no UK speedway fan can ignore, whatever their views on the respective merits of the grand prix system as opposed to a one-off final.

Compared to mid-20th century speedway World Finals, the Cardiff event is very different. The attendance of around 40,000, which exceeds the aggregate weekly turn-out at league tracks throughout Britain, inevitably contains a significant proportion of spectators who are not regular fans, but who treat the event as a big night out of entertainment.

Critics have likened the event to a three and a half hour pop concert, with four heats of speedway inserted into the programme every now and then. One of the major criticisms of the sport aired in the speedway press and on websites is the length of time it takes to run a meeting, and the Grand Prix, largely I am sure due to the demands of live television, is a major instance of this modern day malaise.

Many (again older) fans dislike the constant barrage of very loud music. This is yet another case of moving with the times. The military marching bands and fanfare of trumpeters which were part of the Wembley scene until well into the 1960s would be ridiculed by the vast majority of the Millennium Stadium fans in the second decade of the 21st century.

Taken overall, it is difficult to play down the importance of the Grand Prix-style World Championship to British speedway. It is the one event (apart from a fatality or some wrongdoing on the part of individual riders) which is guaranteed to attract some (although not very much) national media attention.

It plays a major part in ensuring that speedway in the UK retains some credibility. The Millennium Stadium, and Cardiff, are good for British speedway. What a shame that Wales is now without a league track to keep the enthusiasm for the sport alive for more than one evening a year.

Belle Vue Hyde Road

No-one who ever witnessed speedway at Hyde Road will ever forget the experience.

Whether regular supporters of the Aces, or those who simply made a once-a-year pilgrimage to Manchester for the British League Riders Championship Final or other special event, they will always preserve the memory of the unique atmosphere of the stadium.

Grandeur: Belle Vue's legendary Hyde Road Stadium as the fans (from every speedway club in the country) prefer to remember it – packed to the rafters for a British League Riders Championship Final, with the arc lights creating an unforgettable atmosphere. (MKC)

Unique is a much misused word, but it is surely accurate to use it in the context of Hyde Road.

It is very nearly true to say that the stadium was the first to be purpose-built for speedway racing. Almost, but not quite, as the arena was developed on the site of an athletics and cycling track, and the management of the adjacent pleasure gardens, zoo and funfair, intended it to be the home of a professional football team designed to rival the established Manchester giants City and United.

The football project died after a couple of unsuccessful seasons in the obscure Cheshire League, and rugby league was never a huge success at Belle Vue.

Speedway became the venue's raison d'etre and Belle Vue became the world's most famous (and longest-lived) club side, alone in keeping the sport running on a regular basis during World War Two.

It is now a quarter of a century since circumstances forced Belle Vue to quit Hyde Road. Unlike many other teams in a similar situation, the Aces had a ready-made alternative venue just down the road at Kirkmanshulme Lane.

My own first visit to Hyde Road was for a very special match. It was in July 1964, to see Great Britain demolish Soviet Russia 71-37 in the final match of a series of three. It was the first visit of a Russian speedway team to Britain, at a time when the cold war was still pretty icy, and less than two years since the Cuban missile crisis.

Despite the fact that the Russians had lost the opening matches at Wembley and Coventry, there was a tremendous buzz among the crowd. Few of the spectators had ever seen a Russian in the flesh, and the speedway press had built anticipation to fever pitch with their coverage of star men Igor Plechanov, Boris Samorodov and Gabdrakhman 'Gabby' Kadirov, whose Beatle-like hair style gained special attention.

Hyde Road was a pretty-tightly managed set-up. Even with a Control Board all-

Above: Faded glory: Hyde Road, home of the world's most famous speedway team for nearly 60 years, is showing signs of wear and tear as the end draws closer. (KH)

Below: Dereliction: A rainy day in Manchester adds to the sense of desolation as the stadium waits for the arrival of the bulldozers. (EG)

tracks press pass, it was difficult to gain access to the stadium, let alone to the pits. Nothing was allowed to get in the way of running the meeting to schedule and then decanting as many as possible of the thousands of spectators into the funfair, bars, restaurants and dance halls, to put a few more pounds into the Belle Vue coffers.

Another aspect of Hyde Road's uniqueness was the fact that, on several occasions during the speedway season, the track had a more or less captive audience. Belle Vue Gardens was the venue for a wide range of events, from the selection of the national railway queen to religious conventions. In many cases, the trip to the event included an evening at the speedway.

Stadium disasters in the second half of the 20th century, including Hillsborough and the disastrous fire at Bradford City's Valley Parade hastened the arrival of punitive health and safety regulations governing the construction and regulation of sporting arenas.

By the mid-1980s, Hyde Road was getting on for 60 years old. It had been built under a much less strenuous safety regime, and little altered over the years. The closure of the zoo and the funfair had left the stadium isolated, and caused it to be in many ways a bleaker place than in its heyday.

Even if the Hillsborough/Valley Parade disasters had not occurred, the odds are that safety would have been tightened at sports grounds. With its stands constructed almost entirely of timber, and of antiquated design, it is certain that, to survive, the stadium would have needed virtual complete reconstruction at some stage.

Even if any promoter had been in a position to find the necessary funding to transform Hyde Road into a modern arena, it would have probably borne little resemblance to the stadium so greatly loved by speedway fans across the nation and the world.

If and when the new National Speedway Stadium opens just down the road from the old site, I'm looking forward to being on the terraces for the first meeting. It's quite likely that there will be a Russian in the line-up of one or other of the competing teams, this time as an accepted member of the UK speedway family, and not as one of the exotic figures of the 1960s.

Legends in action: Post-war era stars at Hyde Road. Belle Vue and England man Louis Lawson leads Birmingham's Australian test star Graham Warren. (HL)

Glasgow Hampden Park

The tradition of riders being introduced to the crowd and parading around the track prior to the start of a meeting continues today, despite the fact that the often embarrassing size of modern day crowds mean the teams are waving at thin air.

Spare a thought then for the riders who, in an era when speedway was enjoying something of a boom, regularly performed in a stadium occupied by just a tiny fraction of its capacity.

No, not a practice session, but a British League match at Hampden Park. Access was available for spectators only to limited areas of the stadium and the towering terraces on the first and second bends were out of bounds. (PCC)

The picture above was taken at Glasgow's Hampden Park in 1969, not at a practice session, but during a British League meeting. The riders (with the Tigers in the striped race jackets) are taking off from the start line and heading for the first and second turns, overlooked by the truly awesome open terrace behind one of Hampden's goals.

Glasgow moved to Hampden in 1969, after the closure of their traditional base at the White City Stadium. Scotland's national football stadium was then at its peak as far as crowd capacity was concerned and had held an attendance of 149,597 for a Scottish Cup Final some years before.

The Tigers attracted a crowd variously reported as being between 10 and 15 thousand for their opening night at Hampden, a figure which would have meant a tightly packed audience at most speedway venues of the era. At Hampden it represented around 10 per cent of capacity, and for subsequent meetings, this percentage dropped significantly.

When the novelty of speedway in Great Britain's biggest stadium wore off and Tigers attendances levelled off, it was only worth opening limited areas of the stadium, and even then, there was room to spare.

It has to be said that the majority of the riders, both home and away, loved Hampden. Particularly vocal was Kings Lynn captain and international star Terry Betts, who dismissed any suggestion that the vast and empty stands and terraces were a turn-off. Betts said:

How do I fill those terraces? Scottish speedway supremo of the '40s, '50s, '60s and '70s, Ian Hoskins looks out over the cavernous interior of Glasgow's Hampden Park, on the day he signed a deal to re-house the Glasgow Tigers at a stadium then still capable of housing well in excess of 130,000 spectators. (AC)

> I have raced all over the world, but it is great at Hampden. The stadium really is something. It brings out an extra effort from everyone.

Tigers' men Charlie Monk from Australia and Alf Wells from New Zealand had good things to say about the track itself and the speeds that could be reached.

At a time when the changing rooms at some tracks were primitive (to say the least), Wells was even more impressed by the Hampden facilities in this respect.

It's fabulous. More like a luxury hotel than a speedway dressing room. They even have under-floor heating

The Tigers ran at Hampden for four years, before setting off on a true speedway odyssey, that has seen the club operate at no fewer than six venues since departing the giant arena at the end of 1972.

Hampden itself is still the spiritual home of Scottish football, staging international games and cup finals. Just like its English counterpart at Wembley, it has been completely re-developed and is completely unrecognisable from its days as a speedway venue, with a capacity of just above 50,000 people.

The modern-day Hampden Park still has oval-shaped corners. Sadly, these were designed into the refurbished stadium, which now has a capacity of some 52,000 people, to accommodate the 2014 Commonwealth Games. The stadium is the home ground of Queens Park FC, whose average home attendance is less than 1,000. (AC)

When Hampden was redeveloped the stadium retained an oval shape behind each goal, meaning that the fans at each end of the stadium are some way from the football action. Sadly, the shape was retained not to hold out the hope of any future return of speedway, but to facilitate Hampden being used for the 2014 Commonwealth Games in Scotland. The ground will have a much-reduced capacity for the duration.

The temporary exclusion of football from Hampden during the 2014 Commonwealth Games period raises an echo of Edinburgh Monarchs' eviction from Old Meadowbank at the end of 1967 to facilitate the staging of the 1970 version of the same event.

London The White City Stadium

The White City Stadium, a pioneering if intermittent speedway venue, found itself in 1966 at the centre of an incident which illustrates just how much the world of professional sport has changed in subsequent years.

It was the year that the World Cup came to England and when for the first and so far for the only time, as the saying goes, 'football came home' to the nation where it was born.

One of the matches in the tournament, between Uruguay and France, was scheduled for Wembley Stadium, but had to be switched to White City when the Empire Stadium management realised that it would clash with a regular greyhound night and insisted that the dogs take priority.

It must be well nigh impossible for a young sports enthusiast in the 21st century to imagine circumstances in which greyhound racing was given priority over a World Cup football match.

Sadly, it could be argued that the Wembley management's decision to give priority to the greyhound meeting only served to harden the Football Association's dislike of both the dogs and speedway.

The majority of sports journalists and historians are inclined to try to airbrush from the record the substantial influence of greyhound and speedway racing in the 20th century.

The bitter wrangle (still continuing when this book went to press) over the future of London's 2012 Olympic Stadium brings a wry smile to the faces of those speedway fans who know a little about the sport's history. For it was greyhounds and speedway

London's White City Stadium, built as the centrepiece of the Franco-British Exhibition and originally named The Great Stadium, was used for the 1908 Olympic Games. It staged speedway in the late 1920s but the sport's appearances at the circuit were sporadic. The White City was acquired by the Greyhound Racing Association (GRA) who added the all-round roofing and in addition it continued to be a top-class athletics venue. (AC)

which were responsible for saving the bacon not only of Wembley, as recounted on an earlier page, but also of the White City.

The original planning for the White City site envisaged nothing more than a home for the Franco-British Exhibition of 1908, with the name prompted by the steel and concrete construction of the buildings.

The game plan changed radically when Britain, at a late stage, was offered the chance to host the 1908 summer Olympic games, originally allocated to Rome, but switched when that city was unable to raise the finance to build a suitable stadium.

An Olympic Stadium for London was quickly added to the plans for the White City exhibition site, and the arena was built in just 10 months. Different sources give varying capacities for the stadium as originally built, varying from 68,000 to more than 100,000. At the time the World Cup match was played in the mid-1960s the official capacity was 76,567.

The speed of construction of the White City and the quality of its facilities won considerable acclaim. Nevertheless, once the Olympic Games were done and dusted, and for many years to come on both sides of World War One, a more fitting title for the stadium would have White Elephant.

Although the running track continued to be used until 1914, the White City gradually fell into a state of dereliction, from which it was rescued in 1927 by the Greyhound Racing Association.

The all-round roof of the White City as rebuilt by the GRA, and its extensive seating accommodation, made the stadium a suitable alternative venue to Wembley for major events. Pictured here is the trophy presentation for the 1979 World Championship Inter-Continental Final. Michael Lee (centre) took the honours on the day, and is flanked by Peter Collins (left) and Finn Thomsen. (RS)

The GRA developed the arena considerably, constructing additional covered accommodation, with a large proportion seated, and most sports historians now accept that the White City was a forerunner of the modern all-seater stadium.

White City staged speedway for the first time in the pioneering season of 1928. The White City team was a founder member of the Southern League the following year but, unlike at other London venues, the sport failed to establish itself. The stadium continued as a leading greyhound venue, and also staged top-class athletics, professional boxing, rugby league (unsuccessfully) and even American Football.

Despite some sporadic speedway activity in the 1950s, White City was lost to league racing until the mid-1970s, when the Oxford licence was transferred to the venue. From 1976 until 1978, the stadium was home to White City Rebels speedway team, but it proved difficult to attract a paying crowd to regular league meetings.

The stadium was demolished in 1985.

Crystal Palace

Despite its original role as a showcase for what was then ground-breaking technology, any mention of the Crystal Palace today immediately conjures up images of a steam-driven, sepia-tinted Victorian age.

Originally constructed in Hyde Park to house the Great Exhibition of 1851, the constituent parts of the cast-iron and plate-glass marvel were later removed to Sydenham and re-assembled as what would today be called an entertainment complex.

The banking at the Crystal Palace, packed with spectators on this occasion, had unusual wooden crush barriers, barely visible here because of the size of the crowd. Pioneering rider Lionel Wills, who saw the sport on a business trip to Australia in the 1920s and wrote enthusiastic accounts for the British motorcycle press, was no mean rider himself and is pictured well ahead of his opponent. (RFC)

Fashions change whatever the century, and the complex eventually went bankrupt, with the derelict building itself destroyed by fire in 1936.

It could be argued that the true legacy of the Crystal Palace, at least in its South London form, is the role the surrounding grounds and parkland played in the development of British professional sport, including speedway racing.

Crystal Palace was the venue for FA Cup

Crystal Palace promoter Fred Mockford, later to be associated with New Cross, pioneered the starting gate at the South London track. Future New Cross star Tom Farndon, later to be tragically killed on the track, is the rider in the centre. Mockford, in plus fours, developed the gate with rider Harry Shepherd in response to growing concern in the sport about the poor starting techniques originally employed. (CP)

finals, the home of the London County Cricket team, which played first-class matches and was captained and managed by W. G. Grace, and the scene of the first England v New Zealand Rugby international.

The venue's association with some of the greatest early names in dirt-track racing seals the argument in favour of its status as a stately home of speedway, despite the fact that the sport's tenure at the venue was relatively short-lived.

Motorcycle racing came to the venue in the late 1920s, well before speedway's debut at High Beech. Fred Mockford and Cecil Smith successfully promoted a form of mini-road racing called 'path racing', with riders competing on circuits threading through the parkland surrounding what was generally described by the media as 'the Big Glasshouse'.

Speedway pioneer Lionel Wills, an all-round motorcyclist, was among the competitors and was later involved in the moves by Mockford and Smith to transform the former football ground, which had held a record crowd of 121,919 for the 1913 FA Cup final between Aston Villa and Sunderland, into a speedway arena capable of holding more than 70,000 spectators.

Crystal Palace staged open meetings in 1928 and the following year became one of the founder members of the Southern League. In 1932, with many northern clubs folding, that competition became the single section National League.

A handicap for the venue was the lack of track lighting, and at the end of the 1933 season promoters Mockford and Smith transferred the Crystal Palace team to New Cross Stadium.

After the closure for speedway, the circuit was used for midget car racing, with the bikes returning for open licence meetings in the 1936-38 period. A team was entered into the National League Division Two for 1939, but this was not a success and the promoters pulled out in June of that year.

A meeting in 1940 to entertain the troops was Crystal Palace's farewell to speedway. One of the true pioneering venues was to play no part in the sport's golden post-World War Two era, despite a couple of attempts to re-open the track for speedway.

Crystal Palace's most enduring contribution to speedway is the starting gate, a method developed from a horse racing model by Fred Mockford and largely unchanged to this day.

Chapter Three
THE LONDON ARENAS
– Glamour in the Capital City

Hackney Wick Waterden Road

New Cross Stadium Hornshay Street

Wimbledon Plough Lane

Harringay Green Lanes

West Ham Custom House Stadium

With West Ham's Custom House, Harringay and New Cross closed and demolished, and Wembley rebuilt in a manner which excludes the sport, Wimbledon is the only one of the London 'Big Five' to survive in a form capable (at the time of writing) of staging speedway. Plough Lane, as the glass-fronted stands and the GRA symbol on the centre green indicate, is a major greyhound stadium. Gulf Oils was once a major sponsor of speedway. A speedway revival in the early years of the present century failed, and it is likely the stadium itself will disappear altogether. (RS)

LONDON HAS always outshone most if not all of its rivals as a home of top-class sport, with no other capital city matching its half dozen Premiership football teams.

The city dominated speedway at its highest level for long periods of the sport's history. In 1935, at what was arguably speedway's lowest point, fully-professional speedway in Britain effectively consisted of teams from the capital, and Manchester's Belle Vue.

The Aces from the north enjoyed much success in that decade, but for many years after the sport's post war revival in 1946, London imposed an iron grip on speedway's highest honours.

Londoners could watch speedway on every week night, if they were so inclined and their pockets were equal to the expense. Wembley and Harringay in the north of the city, and New Cross and Wimbledon south of the River Thames ensured no-one in the capital was too far from a track, while for a brief spell East Enders could choose between Division One fare at West Ham and second tier thrills at Walthamstow.

The famous 'big five' gave the sport a level of metropolitan glamour that convinced even the most sceptical of sports editors that speedway counted for something.

The only provincial venues that could really compete at the highest level, at a time when most commentators reckoned a capacity of 30,000 was the minimum for top tier racing to succeed, were Belle Vue and the post war era's first new Division One track, at Odsal, Bradford.

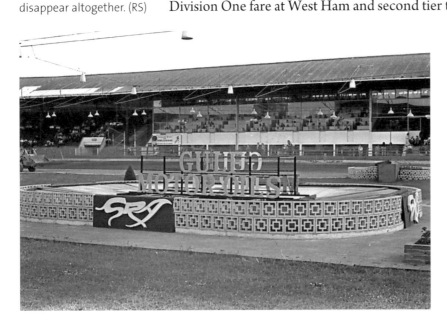

As tracks in three major provincial cities, Birmingham, Norwich and Bristol, became too successful in Division Two for their promotion claims to be denied, the top tier grew to a maximum of ten tracks. London now had to settle for just 50 per cent of the venues at the sport's highest level.

On the track, London continued to dominate absolutely. Every single National League Division One championship, from the revival year of 1946 up to the point in 1957 when the sport's slump forced

The London tracks enjoyed an incredible glamour both before World War Two and in the immediate post-war era, when stars like Cliff Watson of West Ham and 1949 World Champion Tommy Price regularly clashed on track. (AC)

rationalisation into a single league, the championship celebrations took place on a London track.

As the 1950s advanced, this capital city invincibility on the track merely papered over the cracks forming just below the surface.

Crowd levels in the 1940s, particularly at Wembley and West Ham, meant speedway's top tracks were initially able to cope with the punitive entertainment tax levied by the Attlee Labour government from 1945 to 1951, and sustained until 1957 by the Conservatives after they returned to power.

New Cross closed midway through 1953, followed at the end of the 1954 season by Harringay and the London speedway scene would never be quite the same again, despite future revivals.

West Ham could have closed as early as 1952, but the wealthy Alan Sanderson, the man behind successful Division Two tracks at Coventry and Leicester, saved the Hammers at that point. A decade or so later he was to be involved in a further revival at Custom House.

Fellow East Enders Walthamstow had failed to make Division Two speedway a paying proposition in 1950 and 1951, and attempted to persuade the sport's authorities to allow them to take West Ham's place in the top tier. When the attempt failed and the Hammers survived, Walthamstow's management carried out its threat to close down.

Sanderson invested heavily in West Ham, signing World Champion Jack Young from Edinburgh for a record fee, but it was not enough to make the crowds return to Custom House in sufficient numbers. The

The first crack in London's postwar domination of British speedway came in 1953, when New Cross withdrew mid-season from the National League. At the end of the decade Johnnie Hoskins made a brave but ultimately unsuccessful attempt to revive the Rangers. He aimed for the big names to try and draw the crowds to the Old Kent Road track, and is pictured with one of the biggest, Barry Briggs. (AC)

Hammers' withdrawal at the end of 1955 meant that three of the big five had vanished in successive years.

Wembley lasted for a further season, until the premature demise of Sir Arthur Elvin sounded the death knell for the Lions.

Later in the decade, sole London survivors Wimbledon were joined again by New Cross, which re-opened for challenge matches and individual meetings in 1959, and then struggled in the National League for the next two seasons.

The Rangers returned in the Provincial League in 1963, lasting barely half the season, but the same year and the same league saw Hackney Wick operate for the first time since 1939, giving Londoners hope of a capital city revival.

This gathered momentum when the National League promoters, reduced to a rump of six teams by the closure of Southampton, revived West Ham for the 1964 season, with Sanderson and Charles Ochiltree heading the project.

The creation of the British League in 1965, with Wimbledon, West Ham and Hackney competing, allowed the revival of the London Cup and the London Riders Championship. The icing on the cake appeared to be the revival of Wembley Lions in 1970, but this lasted for just two seasons. Worse was to follow, with even the World Final banished from the Empire Stadium after the 1981 event.

Custom House had fallen to the developers in 1972, with the re-located Romford Bombers the final speedway tenants. West Ham's British League Division One licence had been transferred to Ipswich after the 1971 season.

Hackney ploughed on under various promotions, and a massive re-vamp of Waterden Road allowed the venue, in the guise of London Stadium, to stage the first two British Speedway Grand Prix events in 1995 and 1996.

The nadir was reached in the early 1990s. Hackney, after dropping down to the sport's second tier, went out of business in July 1991.

This black year for the capital saw the once dominant Wimbledon Dons, who had also dropped into the second tier National League for the 1985 season, close the doors at Plough Lane. When the sport's two tiers had amalgamated for 1991, Wimbledon opted to race in the top flight, but financial problems meant the team transferred to Eastbourne midway through that season.

There was no speedway in London in the period 1992-1995, although a side known as London Lions, operating at Hackney in its new guise as London Stadium, ran for just one season in 1996.

The final fling for London was the re-opening of Wimbledon in 2002 at the third tier, semi-professional level. That revival, too, ended in tears.

From the complete domination of the post war era to the humiliation of the eventual recognition that the once almighty Wimbledon Dons could attract only a few hundred regular fans to a stadium where, in truth, speedway was no longer really wanted by the greyhound management, represented a savage, if prolonged decline, punctuated by periods of new hope.

Without a doubt, the disappearance of speedway from the nation's capital has seriously damaged the health and the image of the sport.

Hackney Wick Waterden Road

It is a drab, grey sort of day in East London. The year is 1987 and the location is the fading Hackney Wick Stadium, unquestionably the least fashionable of London's classic speedway and greyhound racing tracks, although in many respects perhaps the best loved.

At this point speedway is still just about holding its own at Waterden Road, where even in the boom years of the late 1960s and 1970s management had to work hard to fill the stands and terraces, at a stadium notoriously difficult to access.

Evening greyhound racing has ceased at Hackney, and only a handful of diehard punters are visible in Berris Connoly's superbly evocative photograph. The daytime racing is being staged for the benefit of betting shops throughout the country, a service known as BAGS (Bookmakers Afternoon Greyhound Service), which started in 1967.

No doubt the majority of the punters are keeping warm behind the glass-fronted section of the stand, although a group is clearly visible huddled around the bookmakers' stands next to the start line.

The sparse crowd and crumbling terraces on the first bend indicate a venue in a process of painfully slow but inexorable decline. Yet within just a few years of this photograph being taken, Waterden Road's speedway and greyhound patrons were to experience an amazing sequence of events that at first transformed the venue and then brought about its final demise.

Hackney Wick in 1987, pictured by Berris Connoly during a daytime greyhound meeting, staged almost entirely for the benefit of betting shops, with only a handful of punters present. (BC)

Although Hackney staged speedway racing in the 1930s, the track played no part in the sport's post war boom and did not resurface until Mike Parker launched Provincial League racing in 1963. The irony of 'Provincial' racing in the capital city (New Cross also operated in the league for part of the same season) was much commented upon in the speedway press of the time.

It was not long before speedway at Hackney became inseparable from the name of Len Silver, who moved from Exeter, where he had become a considerable star in the Provincial League, to Waterden Road, initially as a rider and then as promoter.

Hackney survived until 1991 under various managements.

With the greyhounds only stumbling on at Hackney thanks to the BAGS meetings, even the most knowledgeable of greyhound commentators were stunned when plans were announced in the early 1990s for a multi-million redevelopment of Waterden Road.

Many doubts were aired at the time with Hackney's location, always a problem for speedway managements, frequently quoted by the doubters.

The re-vamp, unveiled in 1995, brought fresh hope not just for the greyhound punters, but also for speedway. The refurbished arena coincided with the first season of speedway's World Championship under the Grand Prix format and Waterden Road, re-dubbed London Stadium Hackney, was chosen as the British venue.

In reality, the 'new' Hackney was a white elephant from the start. The company behind the refurbishment went into receivership on the night of the stadium's official opening for greyhound racing.

Team racing returned to Hackney in 1996, courtesy of the London Lions, and the track again staged the British Grand Prix that year. But with attendances for the sport slipping in the UK, and complaints that spectators were largely confined to viewing areas behind glass, the Lions venture proved a failure.

London Stadium Hackney staged just two greyhound meetings in January 1997. Despite rumours of re-opening in the first years of the new century, the bulldozers

moved in during 2003 to clear away the crumbling remains of the new state-of-the art grandstand and the rest of the facilities. The re-vamped venue had lasted for just 14 months.

Although the 2012 Olympics re-generated much of East London, at least in the short term, the attempted regeneration of Waterden Road occurred before new transport links had been completed, which was one of the factors which sealed its eventual doom.

Harringay Green Lanes

The old Wembley was haunted by the memory of the policeman on the white horse on the pitch at the first FA Cup Final, single-handedly holding back a massive and at times unruly crowd, many of whom had broken down barriers to gain admission.

Harringay Stadium's back story also included a memorable appearance by a horseman representing the triumph of good over evil. In this instance he wore not the traditional uniform of a British policeman, but a white Stetson hat, blue jeans and cowboy boots.

Singing cowboy Roy Rogers galloped his Palomino horse Trigger on to the track at Harringay in March 1954, launching a rally staged by American evangelist Dr Billy Graham, with 40,000 boys and girls and 10,000 adults present.

Neither Graham nor Rogers seems to have seen the irony in hiring the North London stadium and its associated arena for a religious event, despite the fact that churches in the UK (and many politicians) were passionate in their opposition to the opening of greyhound tracks in the mid to late 1920s.

Winston Churchill, then Chancellor of the Exchequer, went so far as to describe greyhound racing as little more than 'animated roulette'.

Opponents of dog racing were certainly handed ammunition by events at Harringay. In July 1946 a riot occurred after the disqualification of a dog which had been heavily-backed. Starting traps were burned, restaurants damaged, and the inhabitants of the press box and track officials threatened. When police reinforcements were summoned, they too came under attack.

Speedway was not immune to rioting at Green Lanes. When in May 1938, racing was stopped early due to a crash, some 2,000 members of the crowd demanded their money back. When their demands were ignored they broke onto the track, smashing and damaging parts of the stadium, and setting fire to the tractor.

By the time Billy Graham arrived on the scene, just before the start of the 1954 season, speedway at Harringay was in need of a few prayers.

Harringay was the second of the London Big Five tracks to close to speedway in the 1950s. The stadium, which in subsequent years was used mainly for stock car racing, with the occasional speedway meeting, had an assortment of grandstand styles. Unlike other venues, many standing spectators were accommodated on sloping asphalt banks, rather than on concrete terracing, affecting the viewing potential. (HF)

One of Harringay's biggest crowds of all time was attracted not by Racers' speedway idols such as Vic Duggan or Split Waterman, nor by stock car legends like Jock Lloyd and Chick Woodroffe (later the founder of the Arena Essex Raceway). Spectators, mostly parents and children, poured in to see singing cowboy Roy Rogers and his horse Trigger, who were guests at a religious revival organised by the American evangelist Billy Graham. (HF)

Crowds were falling at Green Lanes and the Racers seemed likely to follow New Cross Rangers, who folded mid-season in 1953, into oblivion.

Billy Graham would not have approved of the fact that a substantial number of Londoners spent Good Friday 1954 not in quiet contemplation, but on the terraces at New Cross watching the birth of British stock car racing.

The consequences for Harringay supporters were dire. After just three meetings at the Old Kent Road track, stock car racing was switched to Green Lanes, which had a bigger track and a larger crowd capacity, despite the fact that much of the standing accommodation consisted not of stepped terracing but merely asphalted slopes.

Speedway crowds had been falling at Harringay and the Greyhound Racing Association, which not only owned Green Lanes but directly promoted the speedway there, staged double-headers to bring what proved to be the Racers' final season to a premature closure, leaving the field clear for the stock cars.

Fred Pallett's picture of Harringay in the 1950s shows the differing architectural styles of the grandstands and also the huge totalisator board. (FPC)

It was not the absolute end for speedway at Harringay. Cavalcade of Speed events, including speedway, were staged in 1958 and 1959, while in 1961 the track was the venue for two prestigious meetings, the Internationale, won by Ove Fundin, and the Provincial League Riders Championship final, won by Reg Reeves.

By the mid-1960s, the speedway track had been covered in tarmac. Ironically, the stock car promoter during that decade was Johnnie Hoskins, 'the father' of speedway racing.

New Cross Stadium Hornshay Street

New Cross Stadium's major bequest to speedway history, thanks to its selection as the principal location for the film *Once a Jolly Swagman*, has proved to be the most evocative surviving image of the sport's golden post war era.

For speedway fans the real stars of the film are the stadium itself and the thousands of genuine New Cross supporters thronging the stands and terraces.

The crowd scenes, for the purposes of the plot set in the 1930s but actually filmed in the immediate post war period (the film was released in 1949), and the style of meeting presentation, with its period announcements and war cries, gives an authentic feel of what it must have been like to have been part of an excited band of supporters at the very height of the sport's popularity.

Less convincing are the members of the cast, particularly matinee idol Dirk Bogarde, surely the most unlikely choice to portray a speedway rider, and Bill Owen, later familiar as Compo in BBC TV's *The Last of the Summer Wine*.

A superb aerial shot of New Cross, showing the rather awkward site the stadium occupied in south London. Railway lines, workshops and housing dictated the design and situation of the grandstands, whilst the terracing on the bends at the top of the photograph had to be squeezed in the middle to fit within the footprint of the stadium. (MKC)

Riders of the era hated the spivvy image of speedway the film depicted, perhaps not helped by the choice of Sid James as the unscrupulous promoter.

The South London stadium, perhaps the least fashionable of the capital city's major stadia, had to be shoe-horned into a very restricted and highly irregular space off the Old Kent Road.

Unlike at other sites developed for greyhound racing, where a considerable acreage of land was cleared for the purpose, the architect of the New Cross arena had to adapt the stadium to fit with the existing infrastructure of factories and terraced houses. At the time it was built, just the width of a railway line separated the dog track from Millwall FC's ground at The Den.

London's other classic greyhound and speedway stadia all had more or less well-defined and geometric shapes. New Cross had bulges in unlikely places, all designed to create the maximum spectator capacity whilst fitting in with existing building lines.

An aerial shot of the stadium shows how the main grandstand was tall and relatively narrow, and how the terracing

A feature of the 1948 film *Once a Jolly Swagman*, largely filmed at New Cross, was the giant spotlight which picked out the riders as they emerge from the dressing rooms to be introduced to the crowd. In the limelight on the hard-surface starting grid in this shot is Old Kent Road idol Ron Johnson. (AC)

virtually disappears on the third bend, where the track is hemmed in by factories, soaring again to a considerable height on the fourth turn, and then ending abruptly before linking up to the main stand.

A close study of the first and second bends also reveal considerable irregularities in the lay-out of the terracing, whilst the covered accommodation on the first bend has a very different shape when seen from the front, compared to the rear view.

No wonder given the limited space available that the length of the greyhound circuit was considerably shorter than at other venues, and that the speedway track, at 262 yards, was in its day the shortest in the UK.

New Cross was a colourful and seemingly permanent part of the British speedway scene from 1934, after promoter Fred Mockford had moved his team from the Crystal Palace, until the Rangers' initial withdrawal from the sport midway through the 1953 season.

Although several other teams had withdrawn from the National and Southern Leagues in the early 1950s (and many more were to follow), the first dent in what had appeared to be the impregnable fortress of London's 'big five' first division tracks shocked the sport.

Mockford blamed several factors, notably the spread of television in that Coronation year and the refusal of the Speedway Control Board to allow him to sign the Swedish star Olle Nygren on a permanent basis.

Britain's first-ever stock car meeting was held at New Cross in 1954 and the venue subsequently pioneered the later Formula Two breed of cars, as seen here. The picture illustrates the size of the covered terrace opposite the main stand. The proximity of the railway is shown by the signal visible above the roof of the building in the top left hand corner of the photograph. (AC)

He also claimed that the scale of the individual popularity of Old Kent Road idol Ron Johnson, whose career had been effectively ended by injury, had been a seriously under-estimated factor in the alarming decline of attendances at New Cross.

The two subsequent speedway re-openings, mentioned in the introduction to this chapter, failed to bring about a long-term revival.

The huge contribution New Cross made to the shale sport has tended to be overshadowed by its role in the introduction of stock car racing, which frightened speedway promoters to death in the mid-1950s, before the likes of Charles Ochiltree at Coventry proved that the two activities could co-exist.

West Ham Custom House Stadium

West Ham's Custom House Stadium is generally remembered for its vast spectator capacity, its fast 440-yard (402 metres) track (up to 1953), at one time made all the more spectacular by its top-dressing of Cornish silver sand, and its fanatical supporters, who in the Hammers' late 1940s heyday numbered 40,000.

To those with an interest in stadium architecture, Custom House will forever be

associated with the work of the celebrated sports ground designer Archibald Leitch. Leitch was a Glaswegian whose first venture into the world of sport came when, in 1899, he was commissioned to design Ibrox Park, the home ground of Rangers FC.

His stadium designs were influenced by his earlier work on industrial buildings and his grandstands, typically with two tiers as at Custom House, were distinguished by their criss-crossed steel balustrades at the front of the upper tier.

Custom House was Leitch's only venture into the world of greyhound and speedway arenas. Fans fortunate enough to have watched racing at the East London stadium will have been aware of the sheer style of the arena, and for later generations this also comes across effectively in photographs.

The shape of Custom House was roughly similar to the original Wembley Stadium, with stands on the home and back straights, curving slightly on to the bends and with graceful pitched roofs.

Wembley's terracing on the bends was considerably more extensive than at Custom House, a fact reflected in the Empire Stadium's ability to hold around 134,000 people, as compared to West Ham's nominal capacity (never completely tested) of around 100,000.

What is difficult to deny is the fact that while the old Wembley had the edge in symmetry, Leitch's two-tier grandstand gave Custom House the most distinctive, grandiose and stylish spectator facility of any speedway venue, ever.

None of the other London arenas could compete with Custom House in design terms. The stands at Harringay and New Cross were essentially an architectural mishmash, and both stadia, impressive as they were in their own ways, looked as if they had been designed and assembled piecemeal.

Wimbledon had the symmetry, with its all-round roof, but this and the terracing and seating it covered were pitched rather too low to be architecturally impressive.

Of the provincial stadia, the wooden stands at Belle Vue's Hyde Road were imposing (and their proximity to the track created a superb atmosphere) but they were in many

West Ham Stadium, built for speedway and greyhound racing with a nominal capacity of 100,000 spectators.

ways insubstantial. Bradford's Odsal and the Alexander Sports Stadium, Birmingham, had extensive open terracing but precious little cover for spectators.

Unlike other stadia, West Ham was designed and constructed with both speedway and greyhound racing in mind. Far from being an afterthought, as was the case elsewhere, speedway actually beat dog racing to the punch at Custom House, with the first meeting taking place a week before the greyhounds' first competitive appearance.

The stadium was big in every sense. The dog track, the longest in the country at 562 yards, allowed a full quarter mile speedway track for much of the Hammers' history.

Association football also featured at Custom House, although the crowds attracted hardly tested Archibald Leitch's grandstand. Thames Association FC, created the lowest recorded attendance in Football League history, when just 469 people turned up for a match against Luton in December 1930.

Not surprisingly, Thames only lasted two seasons in the Football League.

Wimbledon Plough Lane

Fred Pallett photographed the London tracks in the 1950s. As in his earlier shot of West Ham, he has succeeded in capturing the feel of Wimbledon's Plough Lane, with its all-round covered seating and terracing. He has also managed to again include a wooden-bodied truck, evocative of the period. (FPC)

Wimbledon was without a doubt speedway's glamour club in the late 1950s and early 1960s. The Dons, National League champions seven times in eight seasons from 1954 to 1961, were inevitably on fire on their own Plough Lane track and attractive visitors on their travels.

Steered to success by veteran promoter Ronnie Greene, the Dons effortlessly assumed the mantle of speedway's unchallenged aristocrats, following the closure of Wembley as a league venue and the on-track decline of Belle Vue.

The metaphor of the Dons' riders setting the track on fire very nearly reflected reality.

Plough Lane was (and still is at the time of writing) a unique stadium, shaped like an oval shell. The spectator accommodation is covered by an all-over roof

and the terracing that complements the glass-fronted restaurants and bars is of wooden construction.

Former Don Bob Andrews, who rode for Wimbledon during much of the period from 1956 until 1964 recalls an amazing evening at Plough Lane in the late 1950s, when the opposition was provided by a Polish touring team.

As usual, Ronnie Greene was determined to put on a show, as Bob recalls today:

Ronnie arranged for everyone in what was a packed crowd to be given a newspaper on the way in to the stadium.

All the lights were turned off and Ronnie asked everyone to roll up the newspaper, light it and hold it above their heads. There were about 20,000 newspapers alight.

When the newspapers had burnt down to just a short stub, the spectators were supposed to drop them and stamp on them. There were tons of rubbish under the wooden benches and terraces, just as there was many years later at Bradford City's ground, where there was a major disaster.

I still shudder to think what might have happened if a fire had really taken off in a crowded stadium.

What made the incident even more fantastic is the fact that Greene – Ronald W. Greene MBE to give him his full title – had been a senior commander in the London Fire Brigade during World War Two, had been presented to King George V1 when the Monarch reviewed the brigade's despatch riders (organised by Greene) and had been awarded his honour for his work in establishing the service's benevolent fund.

The wide sweeping bends of Plough Lane (and the smartly-dressed start-line staff watching from the centre green, had sadly disappeared by the time speedway was briefly revived at Wimbledon in the first years of the present century. The last speedway track at Wimbledon was very small, situated inside not only the greyhound track but also a stock car and banger circuit. (MMC)

Ronnie Greene's standing with King George V1 paid major dividends in 1946, after the Ministry of Works had refused Wimbledon a licence to render 'first-aid' repairs to their bomb-damaged track lighting system, claiming that the work was 'non-essential'.

Without lights the Dons could not fulfil their league and cup obligations, which would have been a bitter blow to the six-team National League in the sport's post-war comeback season.

As a last resort Greene wrote to the King. Strings were pulled and the licence was eventually granted.

My memories of my only visit to Plough Lane are, like the newspaper lighting incident of the past, potentially inflammatory, at least to died-in-the-wool Dons fanatics.

The Dons had been revived in the third tier Conference League in 2002 and I visited the stadium in 2005. Although the external appearance of the venue looked just as I had always imagined it would, in reality things were very different from the heyday of Ronnie Greene.

The stands and terraces and the well-maintained centre green all tallied with the photographs I had seen of Plough Lane. But my heart sank when I looked at the speedway track, never huge, but now looking miniscule, marooned within its demountable safety fence, inside not only the dog track but also a wide tarmac circuit used for stock cars, bangers and all sorts of odd stunt events (and this at one of speedway's truly aristocratic venues).

The Wimbledon team picture from 2005 shows the temporary safety fence separating the speedway track from the stock car/banger circuit. The wooden terraces have been painted white, with blocks of modern seating. (AC)

The racing was enthusiastic but not particularly interesting, and the dimensions of the track, with tight bends following on from not particularly long straights, appeared to me at least to be at odds with the Conference League's aim of giving young riders plenty of room to make errors and have the space to escape unharmed.

I spent a fair proportion of the evening exploring the stadium, and wondered just how long the speedway revival was going to last (sadly, as it turned out, not much longer).

Although the crowd was well under four figures that evening there was a sizeable number of Wimbledon Stadium stewards on duty at various points of the arena. Meeting the costs involved could not have helped the finances of the new speedway promotion.

Many people will maintain that speedway at any level is better than no speedway at all and no doubt the surviving rump of Wimbledon fans would agree. To the casual visitor such as myself, the evening was a dreadful disappointment.

Plough Lane was the only British speedway home that the legendary Ronnie Moore ever knew, and the place that nurtured Barry Briggs and so many other top class riders. It was the home of The Internationale, a bank holiday individual meeting capable of attracting 20,000 spectators to the stadium in the 1960s.

In retrospect, I wish I had stayed away and relied on the second hand impressions of Plough Lane gained from photographs and old film, rather than having been obliged to witness the grim reality of speedway at the venue in 2005.

POSTSCRIPT: As *Classic Speedway Venues* went to press, various websites were buzzing with speculation regarding the future of Wimbledon Stadium.

Racing Post newspaper reported in July that agreement had been reached between NAMA, Ireland's National Asset Management Agency, and Risk Capital/Galliard Homes to lease the latter company's four GRA greyhound tracks (including Wimbledon) to a team led by GRA managing director Clive Feltham.

The other three tracks whose future has been secured by the deal also include Birmingham Perry Barr (home of Birmingham Brummies), Birmingham Hall Green (a pre-World War Two speedway venue) and Belle Vue Aces' current home at Kirkmanshulme Lane in Manchester.

It was suggested by Racing Post that whilst the new deal gives the two Birmingham venues and Belle Vue leases of up to fifteen years, the Wimbledon lease could be as short as five years. At the same time an Irish businessman was stated to be interested in buying the Wimbledon site, and retaining a greyhound facility. There has been speculation that AFC Wimbledon is interested in acquiring the site of the historic stadium to create a modern football arena, a proposal that has much local support.

It was also suggested that the Irish businessman might, if his bid for the site was successful, look favourably on any proposal to include facilities for speedway within a rebuilt greyhound facility.

Chapter four

PROVINCIAL GREYHOUND STADIA
– Sharing with the Dogs

Belle Vue Kirkmanshulme Lane

Bristol Knowle Stadium

Edinburgh Armadale Stadium

Leicester Blackbird Road

Middlesbrough Cleveland Park

Southampton Bannister Court

Birmingham Perry Barr Stadium

Cardiff White City Stadium

Glasgow White City Stadium

Liverpool Stanley Stadium

Newcastle Brough Park

Wolverhampton Monmore Green

Belle Vue Greyhound Stadium, Kirkmanshulme Lane, is a historic venue both for speedway fans and lovers of dog racing. The stadium staged Britain's first-ever greyhound race meeting in 1926, and also hosted the first season of speedway in the Gorton area of the city, before the opening of the more famous Hyde Road Stadium within the Belle Vue Zoo complex. The GRA's leaping greyhound logo dominates the public face of the stadium. (A)

FROM TIME to time, channel-hopping on television, I flick on to the live greyhound racing coverage, purely for the opportunity to catch a fleeting glimpse of former speedway venues.

Some of the featured tracks, notably Hove Stadium in Sussex and Hall Green in Birmingham, have not staged speedway since the 1920s or 1930s. Others, like Boldon Stadium, Sunderland, have enjoyed a more recent connection with speedway and there are a select few, including Brough Park, Newcastle, where the sport still features.

One of the saddest sights I have seen is the condition of Shawfield Stadium, once the home of Glasgow Tigers and, for one season in the 1990s, the Scottish Monarchs. Shawfield is now Scotland's only licensed greyhound track but, apart from one fairly confined area, its once extensive spectator facilities are visibly decaying and out of bounds to spectators.

Speedway is now in its ninth decade of a pivotal if decidedly uneasy relationship with greyhound racing. It is questionable if speedway would have been able to establish itself in Britain as a fully-professional sport able to cater for large gatherings of spectators had it not been

45

for the availability in 1928 and 1929 of already established and well-appointed greyhound stadia.

In that context, it is notable that the majority of the tracks which survived the end of the pioneering boom to settle down into a small but relatively stable league structure in the latter years of the 1930s were greyhound venues.

Commercial greyhound racing developed from the ancient pastime of hare coursing and first became established as a financial success in Florida, shortly after World War One. Despite image problems resulting from either real or imagined links with mobsters, the sport expanded rapidly and spread to England, when American businessman Charles A. Munn reached agreement with the holders of the patent for the artificial lure.

Munn and his English backers formed the Greyhound Racing Association in 1926 and in the same year constructed the first purpose-built dog racing stadium in Britain, Belle Vue Stadium, Kirkmanshulme Lane, in the Gorton area of Manchester.

Although after a slow start the returns from Kirkmanshulme Lane were encouraging, it must still have been a considerable leap of faith in the period 1926-1928 for the promoters to build tracks in London and the provinces with crowd capacities of up to 100,000.

The gamble nevertheless paid immediate dividends, and greyhound racing thrived for decades. The marriage between speedway and the dogs was consummated in 1928. The attraction was mutual from first sight.

Although greyhound racing customarily took place several times a week, the managements at the new stadia were not averse to the secondary stream of income ground-sharing with the speedway newcomer could produce.

Would-be speedway promoters, imaginations fired by the public response to the sport's High Beech launch, were desperate for ready-made venues.

The speedway promoters, sensing high profits if they were quick enough to cash in on public enthusiasm, were prepared to pay substantial rentals to use the dog tracks. They were also willing to sign contracts which left in the hands of the greyhound managements the not inconsiderable profits which would accrue from speedway crowds using the bars and restaurants at the dog tracks.

For the time being, at least, everyone was happy and making money.

As some of the initial passion went out of the relationship, the dog men and the speedway promoters continued to see the benefits of rubbing along together, despite continual bickering, and the tendency of the greyhound managements to exploit speedway's dependence upon their goodwill by regularly raising the rent.

The speedway promoters consoled themselves with the knowledge that they continued to avoid major capital investment, needing only to maintain their own track surfaces, safety fences, pits and changing rooms, and a few other essentials.

Only in a very few cases did the greyhound managements actually directly promote the speedway, while the construction of purpose-built speedway stadia remained a distinctly rare event, as promoters without a suitable dog track entered into agreements with the owners of football, rugby and athletic arenas.

The greyhound-speedway partnership was an understandable relationship as seen from both sides of the fence, if reflecting a less than ambitious and short-term attitude on the part of the latter sport.

The extent of the sport's dependence upon greyhound tracks at various stages of its development is simple to plot. In 1949, when speedway was at the height of its popularity, attracting more than 11 million people through the turnstiles and again in 1963, when I first began to watch the sport regularly, around 70 per cent of the operating clubs shared their facilities with greyhound racing.

Or, to be more accurate, around 70 per cent of all speedway promotions in the UK were tenants at greyhound stadia, dependent upon the whims of sometimes fickle dog racing managements for their ability to stage the sport.

In 1949 greyhound racing as a major spectator sport probably looked as enduring as the crown jewels. As the post-war recovery progressed, demand for housing and for industrial and commercial units grew significantly and by 1963 greyhound stadia were being seen as attractive prospects for development.

With greyhound crowds starting to decline, the people in control began to be tempted by attractive financial offers.

The last major greyhound track to close its doors in Britain was Oxford's Cowley Stadium, home to speedway from 1949 until 2007. Cowley is shown in happier days. The track lighting, able to be switched to cover either the dog track or speedway circuit, was of a type once familiar. Lighting standards placed at regular intervals between the greyhound and speedway tracks, which can still be found at some shared circuits, can pose a hazard to falling riders. (AC)

Today, the decline of greyhound racing has reached such a level that there are now fewer tracks in the UK as a whole – 25 venues licensed by the Greyhound Board of Great Britain (GBGB) and a few independent or 'flapping' tracks – than the number that used to operate in Greater London alone.

At the time of writing, only ten tracks out of the 28 operating in the Elite, Premier and National leagues stage both speedway and greyhound racing. Apart from Kirkmanshulme Lane, just three of these venues have been shared between the bikes and the dogs since the late 1920s or early 1930s – Newcastle's Brough Park, Sheffield's Owlerton Stadium, and Monmore Green at Wolverhampton.

The decline of greyhound racing, and the subsequent loss of successful speedway clubs, has highlighted the short-sightedness of speedway's close relationship with the

dogs. When the greyhound managements decided to take the money and run, their speedway tenants, still making it pay, had no say whatsoever in the decision.

Speedway in the second decade of the 21st century is no longer beholden to greyhound racing to anything like the same extent as in former years, but teams operating at greyhound tracks must wonder about their security of tenure.

Belle Vue Kirkmanshulme Lane

Kirkmanshulme Lane is (or rather should be) a deeply symbolic place for fans of both greyhound racing and speedway.

The stadium has an unshakeable claim to a place in British sporting history. It staged the UK's first-ever greyhound race meeting in 1926, and a couple of years later was host to the first speedway racing in the Gorton area of the city, before the sport moved down the road to the new Hyde Road stadium, constructed as an integral part of the Belle Vue Zoo Park.

If it was a football, rugby or cricket venue, it would surely be venerated as a place of pilgrimage. Sadly, the reality is

An historic night at Kirkmanshulme Lane as speedway returns for the first time for 60 years to its original Belle Vue venue. The riders return to the pits after the parade, with the now-demolished back straight grandstand forming an impressive backdrop. (CMC)

rather different and for a first time visitor with an interest in the history of both the shale sport and the dogs, it has to be said that it is a downright disappointment.

The loyal but dwindling band of followers of the Belle Vue Aces see it as a facility which, from their point of view, has outlived its usefulness and their focus is firmly on the hope of the proposed new National Speedway Stadium.

Kirkmanshulme Lane today is geared firmly to the needs of the greyhound punters. As at one or two of the UK's other shared venues, watching speedway is not a particularly comfortable experience, unless you are prepared to watch from behind plate glass, and lose much of the atmosphere.

Once inside the quite impressive main building, the corridors and stairways are festooned with posters offering greyhound punters a bargain package combining admission, a meal and a free bet. There is no question as to which sport rules the roost here.

Once inside the spacious grandstand/restaurant/bar area, it is equally obvious that as far as the spectator is concerned, this facility is virtually the one and only impressive thing about Kirkmanshulme Lane today.

There is a paddock in front of the grandstand, stretching the length of the home straight, but the steps are fairly shallow and the view is not tremendous. The rest of what at one time must have been an impressive and commodious stadium has clearly been in decline for many years.

The back straight, which was once the site of a second grandstand, is basically now a void, used primarily as a parking area for riders' vans and cars, as well as forming the pits area for the stock cars which have caused considerable controversy at Kirkmanshulme Lane over the years.

The back straight facilities were demolished for safety reasons and one long-time fan assured me that, towards the end, they had in any case been rat-infested.

There are some steep and extensive open terraced areas on the third and fourth turns, to which speedway spectators are allowed access. Even here, many fans claim that their view of the racing is impeded by the air fence.

> Wherever you stand outside the bar and restaurant, whenever the riders are right in front of you, all you can see is the top of their helmets.

A panoramic view of Kirkmanshulme Lane taken in 1988, after Belle Vue had switched from the doomed Hyde Road. The shot is taken from the extensive terracing on the third and fourth bends, which still exists. Long gone however is the back straight grandstand, visible to the left of the picture. (CMC)

Some of the fans claim that the best viewpoint is a small grassed area on the second bend, close to the large totalisator board.

Disgruntled as many of the Aces fans undoubtedly are, there is nevertheless admiration for the tenacity of the present speedway management in holding on in the face of dwindling crowds and a track which, endlessly pounded as it is by stock cars, is a continuing problem.

The overwhelming feeling is that Kirkmanshulme Lane, despite its history, is a venue which Belle Vue speedway fans will leave with few regrets.

Birmingham Perry Barr Greyhound Stadium

I enthusiastically welcomed the return of speedway to Birmingham in 2007, writing an article proclaiming my belief that the sport's renaissance in England's second city was vitally important to the future of the sport.

I believe fervently that a racing revival in the large urban areas where speedway has thrived in the past is vital if the sport is to regain the credibility it has lost in recent years.

Since the return of the Brummies there have been revivals too in Leicester and Plymouth, and there is hope for the return of racing to Bradford and Norwich.

The current Birmingham promotion scores points in the area where many disillusioned supporters claim speedway as a whole falls down badly – marketing.

I visited Perry Barr on a night when the management sought to boost the attendance with a winning combination of an old-fashioned deal allied to modern technology.

The emblem of the Birchfield Harriers Athletic Club on the façade of the grandstand at the present-day Perry Barr Greyhound Stadium is a reminder that the site previously housed the original Alexander Sports Stadium. (A)

Cut-price admission was available to all comers as long as they first texted their details to the speedway office. When I arrived, the club's enterprise had produced long queues around the stadium, and what was reported as being the best crowd since the 2007 re-opening night.

The innovative marketing also gave the Brummies a useful public relations boost. The track is effectively an island in the centre of a busy road system. Waiting in the queue, it was obvious that many of the people passing by in cars were curious as to what was going on that evening.

Perhaps their curiosity led them to find out about the speedway. Perhaps a few people were persuaded to give it a try themselves.

At least there should be no excuse for people not knowing where the speedway is in Birmingham, despite the complex history of the city's various venues over the years (see the section on the old Alexander Sports Stadium in chapter seven, on page 131).

Suffice it to say at this stage that the present-day Perry Barr Greyhound Stadium is built on the site, and in the footprint of that same Alexander Sports Stadium, legendary home of the Brummies in their post-war glory days.

The impressive glass-fronted grandstand at the present-day Perry Barr Greyhound Stadium, with a large crowd in place for a Birmingham v Wolverhampton Elite League match. (A)

The site of the Perry Barr Greyhound Stadium which was home to the team in the 1970s and 1980s is now a retail park, but is within a stone's throw of the current venue and is a convenient place for speedway fans to park.

Unlike its predecessor, the modern day Perry Barr Greyhound Stadium does not provide a particularly comfortable viewing environment for spectators. The modern glass-fronted grandstand on the home straight is an impressive facility in its own context but, as with Belle Vue's Kirkmanshulme Lane, the context is very firmly that of greyhound racing.

In front of the grandstand is a more or less flat standing area. Away from the region of the grandstand, spectators can only watch racing on the first and second bends. Here the speedway promotion has done the best it can under the circumstances by providing some limited scaffolding and planks-style terracing, which is at least under cover.

It is still something of a puzzle to decide whether the future will bring improvements in conditions for fans at Perry Barr, or whether the fate of the sport, once so popular in the city, will essentially be to cling on with modest crowds in a stadium that only just works as a venue for speedway.

Covered terracing, of a temporary nature, provides limited accommodation for speedway fans on the first bend at Perry Barr. (A)

For all that, I enjoyed an evening's racing at Perry Barr, and certainly plan to return.

Despite the limitations of the present-day stadium for speedway spectators, the place still has a strong sense of its past. Most legendary speedway venues have been replaced by housing, factory units or retail parks. This site, although so vastly changed (and not for the better) still stages speedway.

I felt the weight of history all around me at Perry Barr. For anyone with even a modest imagination, there is a distinct sense of the presence of the Brummie greats of the past, of Alan Hunt and Graham Warren, and perhaps most of all of the 30,000 to 40,000 spectators who used to throng the terraces on this very spot on long-ago Saturday evenings.

Present-day fans might not live in a golden age. That makes it all the more important perhaps to value the speedway we do have.

A postcard view of Knowle Stadium, Bristol, which judging from the pristine condition of the buildings was taken soon after the venue opened for greyhound racing in 1927. The grandstand on the back straight was a victim of a World War Two bombing raid. (AC)

Bristol Knowle Stadium

Speedway in Bristol has succeeded handsomely in the past, and with would-be promoters seeking a suitable new venue, might well flourish once again. Perhaps on a new site the sport in England's sixth largest city may avoid the controversy that was never far away during previous incarnations.

Knowle Stadium, home to Bristol speedway from 1928 to 1960, acquired the dubious distinction in 1951 of being the only known track to reject the chance to stage an official England - Australia test match, one of the sport's most glamorous events.

Bristol boss George Allen shocked the speedway world and dismayed his own fans when he turned down the right to join the exclusive club of test venues.

His Bulldogs side had fought hard to gain promotion to the National League Division One in 1950, winning back-to-back Division Two titles and mounting an intensive lobbying campaign. Sanctioning Bristol's promotion seemed to confirm that the Control Board and other promoters accepted Knowle's status as a suitable venue for top flight racing.

Allen, still angered by the initial refusal to promote Bristol and the lack of help he received in team-building, was consistently outspoken. No-one in the sport, however, expected him to give the thumbs down to the offer of a Lions – Kangaroos test, made at the promoters' pre-season meeting.

The supporters were distraught, but Allen was adamant, describing the Knowle facilities as offering 'poor accommodation'.

National League Division Two match race action on the tight circuit at Knowle in 1948, as home star and current holder of the title Fred 'Friar' Tuck attempts to block the progress of Wilf Jay of Newcastle. Jay's challenge was successful, with the Newcastle man winning on the night by two races to nil. (JFC)

Bristol was extensively bombed during World War Two. Although Knowle was three miles outside the city centre, it lay within a target area, close to Bristol's Whitchurch Airport, virtually the only facility in Britain offering civilian flights during the war years and also a hub for ferrying fighter and bomber aircraft to operational stations.

The area was duly raided and Knowle Stadium sustained bomb damage, including the loss of one of its three modestly-sized grandstands.

George Allen argued that staging such an important fixture as a test match needed the best accommodation, saying:

> We have been allowed no building permits to repair our bomb-damaged track. It is useless to try and stage such a match without properly-covered enclosures and stands and we have been waiting for years to get the permits through.

Despite healthy crowds and covered accommodation on the home straight which survived the war years, the Bristol management angered their fans by turning down the chance of an England-Australia test match, on the grounds that the facilities at Knowle Stadium were inadequate. (AC)

The fans were annoyed and sceptical of the promotion's claims to have made attempts to improve facilities, pointing out that Bristol City Football Club had recently been able to construct a new stand.

Looking back, George Allen's decision appears strange. Knowle at the time claimed an estimated capacity of 24,000, and had housed a crowd of around 22,000 for a match against Belle Vue in May 1949. Attendances at test matches had started to decline by 1951 and the England-Australia clash at Odsal in June attracted 27,780 spectators, a figure not that much higher than might have been accommodated at Knowle.

Bristol *did* stage an official test match in September 1953, when a reported 12,000 spectators (and BBC TV viewers) saw England beat New Zealand 77-31.

Controversy again reared its head at Knowle at the end of the 1953 campaign, when the Bulldogs' 'voluntarily withdrew' from Division One after finishing bottom of the table. George Allen was a bitter man, claiming the Bulldogs had struggled to gain any assistance when it came to signing riders.

Although the Bulldogs won a third post-war Division Two championship in 1954 (the team had won the Provincial League in 1937), interest was declining rapidly and there was no question this time of seeking promotion. Midway through 1955 Bristol withdrew from Division Two.

Knowle staged another season of speedway in 1960, when the Bulldogs finished third in the inaugural Provincial League. The stadium was then sold for housing.

Bristol's most recent speedway was staged in 1977/78 at Eastville, home of Bristol Rovers FC and greyhound racing. The venture, equally, if not more controversial, than the Knowle experience, was a success from a crowd point of view, but ended in tears when anti-noise protesters carried the day.

Cardiff's White City Stadium was effectively driven out of business as a greyhound racing venue by the introduction of dog racing at the old Arms Park rugby ground in the city centre, which was eventually replaced as the national stadium of Wales by the Millennium Stadium. The pattern of a number of small wooden grandstands around the perimeter of the track, to supplement a much more substantial main facility, was common to a number of shared greyhound/ speedway venues. (NMW)

Cardiff The White City Stadium, Sloper Road

Wales is truly a land of myth and legend, with speedway racing in the principality having its fair share of tall tales.

Speedway in Wales today is a once-a-year event, confined to the British Grand Prix in Cardiff. Just like many of the mythical places and characters in the country's rich heritage of folklore, it appears for a day and then vanishes for twelve months, in the true Celtic tradition.

Many of the thousands who pour across the Severn for the Grand Prix are probably only vaguely aware that speedway in Wales dates back to the very early days of the sport in the British Isles.

Speedway at Cardiff's White City Stadium can claim (if only just) to have begun during the sport's initial UK season of 1928, with the first meeting taking place on Boxing Day that year.

The Stadium, in the Grangetown district of the city at Sloper Road, had been opened by the Greyhound Racing Association in April 1928. Having tested the waters at an earlier stadium in Grangetown, the GRA invested heavily in the construction of the White City.

Photographs of the venue show a very substantial main grandstand on the home straight and no fewer than six individual stands along the back straight and around the third and fourth bends, together with some substantial open terracing. The first and second bends have only rough banking, with a totalisator board at the apex.

The point where myth creeps in to the White City story comes between the official opening for greyhound racing in 1928 and the first speedway meeting at the end of the year.

Rugby League has made continual attempts over the decades to convert the Union-playing Welsh to the 13-a-side code. It has been claimed that, on 14 November 1928, 70,000 spectators attended a Wales versus England rugby league international at the White City.

Looking at the aerial photographs of Sloper Road, it is difficult to imagine a crowd of that size fitting into the venue, and other estimates of the nominal capacity of the stadium seem to suggest an upper limit of around 40,000.

A careful search through rugby league records confirms that a match between the two sides did take place, resulting in a 39-15 win for England, but the best estimate of the attendance puts it at around 15,000. Greyhound racing proved popular initially at the venue, with reports suggesting that around 20,000 people paid to see the legendary greyhound Mick the Miller win the Welsh Derby in 1930.

Speedway was not an unqualified success in Cardiff. Although reports speak of 25,000 people at the White City for the first meeting, and notwithstanding the fact that the promoters staged no fewer than 55 meetings in 1929, interest tailed off in 1930 and there was no racing at all in the subsequent three seasons.

The sport returned for just one meeting in 1934 and in the following year there was some investment in the track by the stadium owners. When the Provincial League was launched in 1936 Cardiff were founder members, but failed to complete the season. A further one-off meeting the following year failed to re-ignite interest.

The White City was sold in 1939 to the steel firm Guest Keen and Nettlefolds for use as a company sports ground. With the decline of the industry in South Wales, in 1984 the site became the inevitable housing estate.

Edinburgh Scotswaste Arena, Armadale

Britain's newest speedway tracks tend to be situated in areas carefully chosen to please the planners and avoid damaging claims that the noise of the bikes and the loudspeakers blight the lives of nearby residents.

Venues developed in the 21st century (and some of the tracks with a much longer history) are situated in rural surroundings, or occupy tucked-away sites on industrial estates, where most of the daytime inhabitants have long headed for home by the time the machines start to warm up.

Armadale Stadium, the Scotswaste Arena, situated some 20 miles south of Edinburgh city centre, may be a 'flapping track' in greyhound parlance, largely built of wood and corrugated iron, but the speedway management goes to considerable lengths to keep the venue trim, as evidenced by the immaculate centre green and general air of tidiness. (A)

It naturally comes as something of a shock to realise that Edinburgh Monarchs' home at the Scotswaste Arena in West Lothian, some 20 miles from Scotland's capital, is surrounded on three sides by new housing, coming right up to the boundary of the small and homely venue.

In the circumstances it is encouraging to be told by Monarchs' director and co-promoter John Campbell:

> We have not had a single complaint from a local resident about noise from the speedway. One or two grouses about parking perhaps, but noise has not been an issue.

Modern housing has gradually been developed on three sides of Armadale Stadium, with dwellings just behind the covered area on the home straight. (A)

Above right: The small covered stand on the third and fourth bends, which has a mix of seating and standing accommodation, is a popular spot with Edinburgh fans. (A)

It may be that one factor that contributes to the generally satisfactory relationship between the speedway and planners and residents is the fact that planning consent for stock car racing at Armadale imposed virtually no restrictions on the number of meetings that could be held.

The stock cars are gone from the venue, although the extended track used by that sport is still visible at the pits end of the stadium. Locals no doubt feel that the relatively short speedway meetings, with the sport's present-day controls on noise, is definitely preferable to the stock cars.

Armadale is not the most elegant stadium in speedway, with wood and corrugated iron the most common building materials. In greyhound parlance it is a 'flapping track', one of only four circuits (one, the former speedway venue at Shawfield in Glasgow is registered and three are independent), still staging dog racing in Scotland.

The venue has the merit of having given the Monarchs some much needed stability. In the half century since the Provincial League brought the sport back to the capital, the team has operated at four venues.

The club's spiritual home at Old Meadowbank was destroyed to build a new stadium for the 1970 Commonwealth Games (see page 74), and the Albion Rovers football stadium at Coatbridge lasted for only a couple of seasons before the British League Division One licence was transferred to Reading.

The historic Powderhall Stadium was home from 1977 to 1995, while a fifth venue, Shawfield, hosted a team called the Scottish Monarchs in 1996, before the Edinburgh name was revived at Armadale.

Monarchs have been linked to a move to the Royal Highland Centre at Ingliston, close to Edinburgh airport and about 11 miles west of the city. John Campbell acknowledges that interest in Ingliston is still alive, but is cautious about the prospects.

We would like to move to a venue that is much closer to the city, but the position at the moment is that the ball is in the Royal Highland Centre's court. As a showground venue, I would say it is better than Peterborough, with a main show ring with a grandstand and a huge bar and hospitality area.

In the meantime, we do what we can at Armadale.

Despite the fact that Armadale's future as a sports stadium is not wholly secure, the Monarchs' management actually do a pretty good job of presenting speedway in the arena.

Armadale has plenty of cover available for spectators along the home straight, and the facilities include an attractive bar, decked out with speedway memorabilia. The covered terracing on the third and fourth bends is popular with supporters and gives a good view of the racing.

Glasgow White City Stadium

Perhaps in centuries to come archaeologists will excavate a variety of sites and find traces of a sport which in its heyday gripped the imagination of millions of 20th century citizens of Great Britain.

They will certainly have a wide variety of locations for their digs, with former speedway stadia lying buried beneath housing estates, industrial complexes, and retail parks, to say nothing of sporting venues such as the London 2012 Olympic Games site in east London (formerly Hackney Wick Stadium) and the Commonwealth Games Stadium in Edinburgh (Old Meadowbank).

Perhaps the strangest fate to befall a speedway venue was the closure and demolition of Glasgow's White City Stadium, to accommodate the construction of the M8 motorway.

It is ironic, given that the motorway system as a whole greatly improved the travelling experience for speedway riders around the country and greatly eased communications between England and Scotland.

When Trevor Redmond, better known for promoting speedway and stock car racing in the south west of England, became the front man at White City in 1964, working in association with Ian and Johnnie Hoskins for a new Provincial League promotion, the vast majority of riders were based in England, particularly in London and the south of the country.

Redmond's team-building plans included flying former Southampton and Coventry rider Maury Mattingly from his Hampshire home to White City every week.

White City, situated on Paisley Road West in Ibrox, Glasgow (close to Rangers FC's Ibrox Stadium), was opened for greyhound racing in April 1928 and staged a single speedway meeting in June of that year. After a full season of open licence events in 1929 Glasgow competed in the Northern League in 1930 and 1931.

Midget car racing took place at the stadium in 1937 and 1938, with speedway

Glasgow White City Stadium, demolished to make way for an urban motorway, was typical of the bigger greyhound stadia found in major cities. The main grandstand, illustrated here, stretched the length of the home straight, while back straight fans also enjoyed covered accommodation. (PCC)

Start line action from a Glasgow versus Cradley clash, with the white-shirted Cradley star Ivor Brown on the inside. The extensive covered terracing on the back straight was appreciated by the fans on colder evenings. (PCC)

The landmark of the tote board provided a meeting point at White City for regular fans. (PCC)

returning in 1939, when a Glasgow team competed in the Union Cup. Six open licence meetings were staged in 1940 and Glasgow was quick to resume after the end of hostilities, with an open meeting in 1945 and a place in the Northern League in 1946. Ian Hoskins, demobilised from the RAF, promoted in association with father Johnnie.

Although speedway at White City was initially very successful, particularly when the launches of Edinburgh Old Meadowbank, Glasgow Ashfield and Motherwell created real Scottish rivalry, the sport's mid-1950s' slump claimed the Tigers early in the 1954 campaign, before any league matches had been ridden.

There were a couple of attempts at revivals before the 1964 Provincial League start-up. The Tigers' eventual eviction from White City led to a nomadic existence, not dissimilar to that experienced by the Glasgow side's great rivals from Edinburgh.

Glasgow had a four-year spell at Hampden Park (see page 27), a similar tenure at the Coatbridge venue vacated by rivals Edinburgh a few years earlier, spells at Blantyre Sports Stadium and later (after being the victims of another road building project) at Craighead Park, Blantyre.

After a rather bizarre spell racing at Workington, the Tigers moved back to the city of Glasgow, to the well-appointed Shawfield Greyhound Stadium

The final move (to date) came in 1999, with a switch to Saracen Park, Ashfield, formerly the home track of early 1950s rivals Ashfield Giants (see page 78).

Leicester Blackbird Road Stadium

The half-timbered effect gave a stately appearance to the façade of Leicester Stadium, and double-world champion Jack Young compared the grandstand entrance facilities to those of a plush cinema. The stadium is long-vanished, as is the likelihood of seeing a policeman, complete with white armbands, on traffic point duty. (AJC)

They say you never really value something until it has gone. No doubt many East Midland speedway and greyhound racing fans took Leicester's Blackbird Road for granted during the years when it seemed a permanent fixture of the local sporting scene.

Once the doors had closed for the final time, the city realised just what a superb sporting facility had been lost for ever.

I believe there are ample reasons for regarding Blackbird Road as the sport's provincial lost theatre of dreams – and I say that without meaning any disrespect to Leicester's excellent new venue at Beaumont Park (see page 103).

Anyone who sampled the atmosphere of Blackbird Road during a Midlands derby match against Coventry, with a five figure crowd and

The interior of Blackbird Road, seen from a vantage point close to the totalisator board illustrated in the introduction to this chapter on page 48. The grandstand and the extensive terracing all around the stadium were supplemented by a smaller area of cover on the fourth turn. (RS)

the sort of tension you could cut with a knife, will surely nod their head in agreement with my enthusiasm for the historic home of speedway in Leicester.

Don't just take *my* word when it comes to recalling Leicester's magic. The first person to draw an analogy with the theatrical splendour of the vast, terraced bowl of a stadium, who instinctively grasped that Blackbird Road was virtually unsurpassed as a grand stage for the most spectacular of all sports, was Australian double world champion Jack Young.

Young paid his first visit to Blackbird Road with Edinburgh Monarchs in 1951, the season that culminated in his first World title. Leicester had just been promoted to the National League Division Two and Blackbird Road instantly struck a chord with the rider.

South Australian Young was noted for his lively interest in his surroundings and his colleagues during the ten seasons he spent in British speedway. Even before the first of his two World Championship victories, he was identified as a natural subject for a weekly (presumably ghost-written) magazine column.

This comes across today as one of the best of its kind and must have owed as much to Young's observations of the British speedway scene as it did to the writing skills of the ghost.

Jack Young's early British experience with Edinburgh, and subsequent transfer to West Ham, meant that by the mid-1950s, unlike some of the sport's top-notchers, he had experienced a wide variety of tracks in both Division One and Division Two (with some of them in the lower tier leaving something to be desired when it came to the quality of facilities for both riders and spectators).

Young was deeply impressed with not only the racing conditions at Blackbird Road, but also with its towering terraces and well-laid out grandstand. He wrote:

> I like the appearance of the place. It must make spectating a real treat for the customers.

The early 1950s was the heyday of the super cinema, and Young found the same sort of luxurious surroundings laid on for the Leicester fans who patronised the Blackbird Road grandstand, with its mock Tudor main façade. His judgment, quoted in his weekly column, was:

It's like going into a picture palace when you enter the stand.

My own experiences at Blackbird Road encompassed the stadium at its best and also at its worst.

My first experience was on a dark autumn evening during Leicester's disastrous 1962 Provincial League season. The crowd of perhaps eight or nine hundred people, watching another home defeat, were mostly huddled under and around the grandstand. The looming terraces on the back straight, barely visible in the shadows beyond the track lighting, were empty and desolate.

My next visit, six years later, after Long Eaton's British League licence had been switched to Blackbird Road, revealed a far different picture.

On a spring evening, at the start of a new and prosperous era for Leicester, the start of the meeting was delayed for an hour as considerably more than ten times the number of spectators who had been present for my first visit packed the stadium.

That sort of attendance and the resulting magical atmosphere would have been the norm during Jack Young's earliest visits to Blackbird Road. The crowds were to again decline before the stadium fell victim to redevelopment in 1984, but like Young, I believe I saw and experienced the venue at an inspiring peak.

The Leicester revival in the British League in 1968 – the licence was transferred from Long Eaton – was a huge success. One of the men signed to augment the former Archers' side was John Hart, pictured leading opponents from one of his former clubs, Cradley Heath. (AC)

Liverpool Stanley Stadium

Speedway's failure to establish itself on Merseyside is one of the more baffling aspects of the sport's history in the UK.

Liverpool is not unique in its status as a major provincial city which has for the most part shunned the attractions of the shale sport. Leeds, its great rival on the football field in past decades and Cardiff, where the success of the British Grand Prix only serves to emphasise the utter failure of league racing in the city, are the other prime examples.

Stanley Stadium, situated off the Prescott Road in Liverpool, was an early greyhound venue, opening in August 1927 barely a month after the first British dog meeting at Belle Vue's Kirkmanshulme Lane.

Rows of terraced houses, hair shiny with Brylcreem and female supporters with headscarves give an authentic period feel to this late 1940s shot, taken from the viewpoint of the terrace fan, at Liverpool's Stanley Stadium. The sign on the end of the main grandstand reads 'Stanley Greyhounds'. (RDC)

As far as speedway, first introduced a year later was concerned, the track fitted into a pattern familiar in the north of England in the late 1920s and the 1930s. Initial boom, a couple of seasons in the English Dirt-track and Northern Leagues, and a spell in the first Provincial League in 1936-37, which came to an end midway through the latter year when E. O. Spence of Belle Vue, who had taken over the running of the track, transferred the remaining fixtures to Hyde Road.

Southern Speedways, run by Jimmy Baxter, with Gordon Parkins (later associated with Norwich) as manager, re-opened at Stanley in 1949, at first in Division Three of the National League and later in Division Two.

Rider Reg Duval experienced life at Stanley Stadium on both sides of the safety fence. He rode for the Chads team from 1949 to the end of the 1952 season. The Chads, named after a cartoon character, had only limited success on the track, always occupying a place in the lower part of the league table.

The Stanley track was one of the biggest in the country, varying between 432 yards in the early 1930s to a massive 446 yards in the later 1950s. Reg Duval explained:

> It was an easy track to ride, perhaps too easy where the interests of the Liverpool riders and fans were concerned. There was no home advantage at all and quite a lot of home matches were lost, which is never a good thing.

Duval left Stanley Stadium at the end of 1952, joining Coventry, which was closer to his London home.

As the fifties decade drew on, he sensed that a Liverpool revival might prove successful.

> I reasoned that the track had had a break since 1953 and I also believed I could run it successfully by being on the spot. I always believed that Jimmy Baxter had been at a disadvantage being based in London. The crowds responded well and it could have been a big success.
>
> What I didn't bargain for was the absolute hostility I faced from the

Stanley's inner-city location on the Prescot Road in Liverpool is evident in a shot taken from the main grandstand, of riders on parade for a World Championship qualifier – no identification problems here. The smaller stands around the perimeter are of a common design once also found at Cardiff White City, Newcastle, Long Eaton and elsewhere. (RDC)

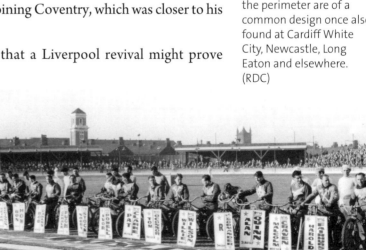

other promoters. Although when I launched the track I had a good idea that the crippling entertainment tax was likely to be reduced, I didn't think it would be removed altogether.

The other promoters looked upon me as someone cashing in on the removal of the tax. They thought it unfair that after they had struggled through the mid-fifties slump, this character was going to come along and make a fat profit.

Reg Duval still believes his experience at Liverpool represented a lost opportunity for British speedway.

To me the Provincial League that arrived three years later lowered the standard, at least until the British League came along. The PL has been described as being the saviour of British speedway but it used has-been and never-beens as riders. I wanted to run Liverpool using the best riders available, and start a revival at the top level.

It seems the Merseyside supporters agreed with his point of view. Although attendances for Mike Parker's 'pirate' meetings in 1959 were encouraging, the single season of Provincial League racing at Stanley Stadium in 1960 was a flop.

That was the end of speedway on Merseyside, and with the stadium gone, a revival after more than half a century seems highly unlikely.

Liverpool was the home town of double World Champion Peter Craven and he made some appearances for the Merseyside team before transferring to Belle Vue and glory. (RDC)

Middlesbrough Cleveland Park

Speedway loves its myths and legends, even on the occasions when they seem to have little basis in reality.

Self-pronounced purists rather dislike the racer (no pun intended) show business

side of the sport. They are speedway's disapproving roundheads, as opposed to the dashing cavalier riders and promoters who over the years have brought such colour and spectacle to the lives of the majority of fans.

For more than six decades speedway on the banks of the River Tees, traditionally (and now once again) part of the ceremonial county of North Yorkshire, despite the attempt to rebrand the area as Tees-side, was based at Cleveland Park.

The legend surrounding the Middlesbrough Bears was that the track, one of the original 12 venues to re-introduce league speedway in 1946, was forced to close its doors after just three seasons because the team was too good!

Without the stringent rider control measures of the present day, calculated on points averages, the Bears management voluntarily broke up their team in a bid to reduce the number of runaway victories at Cleveland Park that were apparently driving the fans away.

Speedway came to Cleveland Park in August 1928, initially under the direction of Johnnie Hoskins. Like so many provincial circuits, the track experienced many ups and downs during the 1930s, but was quick to re-open after World War Two, staging open meetings in 1945 and joining the second tier Northern League for 1946.

Success, elusive during the 1930s (the team was bottom of the English Dirt-track League in 1929 and resigned prematurely from National League Division Two during its only other pre-war taste of competitive racing in 1939) was now instant.

Middlesbrough romped home to the Northern League title in 1946, finishing five points clear of Sheffield, and repeated the success in 1947, again pipping Sheffield to the post.

The Bears' fans had to be content with third place in Division Two in 1948, but by that time the numbers in the stands and the terraces at Cleveland Park had diminished rapidly.

Middlesbrough were an exceptionally powerful side in 1947, with the Division Two averages topped by Frank Hodgson and Wilf Plant, with Kid Curtis not far behind. At the start of the 1948 season Middlesbrough were theoretically a weaker side than during the previous campaign, having exchanged the highly popular Curtis for West Ham reserve Benny King.

The 1948 campaign at first looked like it would be an enhanced replay of the previous year. The Bears looked again to be a strong team and a record crowd of 15,906

A close-up of the start line at Cleveland Park shows the glassed-in frontage of the main stand and the terracing underneath. The small structure with signage pointing to the tote facilities provided extra cover for patrons. (RN/RSO)

Above left: The lifting bridge over the River Tees visible in the background is still evident today, more than can be said for Middlesbrough's Cleveland Park Stadium. The two grandstands of similar construction were augmented by covered terracing on the back straight. (RS)

Provincial League speedway at Middlesbrough in 1964. The ever-popular former Belle Vue rider Maurice 'Slant' Payling, transferred from Long Eaton, another track run by promoter Reg Fearman, is on parade with another former Archer, Eric 'Bluey' Scott. (RN/RSO)

flocked to Cleveland Park for the opening meeting against Sheffield.

The steel town team, the strongest challengers to the Bears in the previous two seasons, were casually brushed aside by 51 points to 33. The following week, when Glasgow were thrashed 61-22, the crowd had fallen to 6,200.

The Bears scored more than 60 points in a home match on four occasions in 1948 and routinely had a winning margin of between 15 and 20 points, losing twice (to eventual champions Bristol and runners-up Birmingham) at Cleveland Park, after the team had been deliberately weakened by the transfer of Wilf Plant to Fleetwood.

At the end of the 1948 season, there was a round of speedway musical chairs, with the Middlesbrough team moving to Newcastle and the Tyneside men being switched to Johnnie Hoskins new track at Glasgow Ashfield.

The well-appointed Cleveland Park, with two sizeable grandstands on the home straight and the fourth bend, and cover all along the back straight, was not to see league racing again until Provincial League action began in 1961.

Was the strength of the Bears and the frequency of runaway home victories the sole reason for the decline of the crowds at Cleveland Park in the 1940s? Not necessarily.

Post-war prosperity in Britain was patchy, with some regions recovering from austerity much quicker than others.

In the period from 1947, when speedway was in the ascendancy, to the end of 1951, before the sport's slump had resally gathered pace, the north of England saw proportionally more track closures than elsewhere. Wigan, Wombwell, Middlesbrough, Hull, Sheffield, Newcastle and Halifax all closed their doors.

League speedway in the north of England was to be decimated before the Provincial League revival, with Belle Vue the sole survivor by 1958. The loss of Middlesbrough a decade before can be seen as a precursor of the rout.

Newcastle Brough Park

Brough Park, once one of the sport's most iconic arenas, is now a classic example of the great shrinking speedway stadium.

Home to greyhound racing since 1928, with speedway first introduced a year later, the venue now officially known as Newcastle Stadium is famed not only as one of the few remaining tracks from the pioneer era of the sport, but also for its status in the 1960s and 1970s as the home of World Championship legends Ivan Mauger and Ole Olsen.

Diamonds fans have seen the best in their time, but have also seen the amenities at Brough Park and the profile of the stadium in the community contract significantly.

Today, like another pioneering venue, Monmore Green, Wolverhampton, viewing is restricted to the home straight terracing and the glass-fronted bar/restaurant areas – all that is needed for greyhound racing crowds and, to be absolutely fair, sufficient to accommodate the average speedway attendance in the 21st century.

George English, co-owner and co-promoter of today's Diamonds, was a fan on the terraces at Brough in the 1960s. He has seen the stadium diminish in size over the years, as he explains:

> It used to be an all-round stadium, with the entrance in a prominent spot at the top end of the Fosseway, where an industrial estate stands now. You used to walk through gardens to get to the track.
>
> The back straight, with a second sizeable grandstand, was still in use up to approximately 1991. Then the whole area was closed and the back straight stand demolished.
>
> There were also smaller covered stands on the third and fourth bends, separated by the Tote board. As a youngster in the early 1960s I used to watch the racing from a wooden stand.

The speedway promotion and the fans were dealt a blow just before the start of the 2013 season when they were informed by the owners of the stadium that the terracing below the overhang of the glass-fronted grandstand had been declared unsafe, due to major cracks appearing in the concrete.

On my visit to Newcastle the terracing under the overhanging roof of the surviving grandstand, offering the only cover for supporters who prefer not to view racing through plate glass, was cordoned off. George English explained:

> The covered accommodation outside the stand is is far more important to the speedway than it is to the greyhounds. The stadium owners carried out the necessary repair work, but at their pace, which didn't help us at all.

At the start of the 2013 season, during a cold spring, the upper part of the terracing at Newcastle was closed by the stadium owners after major cracks had appeared in the concrete, leaving the outdoor speedway spectators without any covered accommodation. (A)

Above left: Brough Park is an historic but significantly diminished shared venue, now re-named Newcastle Stadium by the company which owns the arena and promotes the greyhound racing. The only remaining spectator facilities at the venue are the main stand on the home straight and the terracing in front and to the side. (A)

The back straight at Brough Park is now closed to spectators, with the former stand and other accommodation demolished. (A)

The wooden stands from which current Newcastle promoter George English first watched speedway, on the third and fourth bends at Brough Park, are clearly visible in this 1947 picture, together with the large totalisator board. Newcastle rider Wilf Jay is clearly delighted to receive a trophy from a distinguished visitor, the American James Baskett, who played the character of Uncle Remus in the 1946 Walt Disney film *Song of the South*. (JFC)

With the remaining grandstand re-clad, you need to look fairly closely to detect any original touches at Brough Park. The most obvious are the highly decorative ceilings on the ground floor of the grandstand, which houses a bar and other refreshment and betting facilities.

The venue must have been quite some place in its heyday. Thanks to dedicated owners and a loyal bunch of supporters, Brough Park is still an important part of the speedway family – with what must be the finest (and very reasonably-priced) programme in the sport.

It is important to the sport as a whole that Newcastle continues to thrive.

Southampton Bannister Court

There was a time, before speedway and many other professional sports at the highest level became largely the preserve of overseas performers, when local pride was at the very heart of a club or promotion.

Few if any speedway ventures had such a strong local background as Southampton. From the sport's UK birth in 1928, through successive eras of boom and bust, speedway in the south coast port was associated with the Knott family, and in particular with Charles Knott Senior.

Charles Knott was born in the dockland heart of Southampton in 1891, to a family with deep roots in the town. His family background was modest, and as a boy he sold bags of sweets to theatre queues.

His entrepreneurial skills allowed him to develop a business selling fish, fruit and other goods, first from a handcart, then from a pony and trap, and later from a market stall, laying the foundations of a substantial retail and wholesale fish business.

His great interest, outside of family life, was in sport. In 1927 he bought land at Bannister Court, next to Hampshire County Cricket Club's ground at Northlands Road,

The much-mourned Bannister Court at Southampton was at the centre of a major sports complex. At the top left is part of the old Hampshire County Cricket Ground, where Charles Knott Junior, son of Southampton founder Charles Knott, took many wickets for his home county. An adjacent ice rink was owned by the Knotts and the circuit inside the speedway track was used for roller derby events. (MKC)

to build a greyhound stadium, with the first meeting taking place in August 1928.

The whirlwind rise of speedway racing that same year led him to incorporate a dirt track, with speedway making its debut on 6 October 1928.

Bannister Court Stadium stood at the centre of a veritable sports complex. Charles Knott was quick to grasp the significance of the new sports and pastimes gaining in popularity in an era which, sometimes confusingly, encompassed both industrial depression and also growing leisure opportunities for ordinary people.

In addition to the greyhound and speedway tracks, the latter the home to the Southampton Saints team, founder members of the Southern League in 1929 and runners-up in both that year and in 1930, the stadium incorporated an inner circuit for roller skating and areas for roller hockey and tennis.

A decade later, Charles expanded the business, buying Southampton Sportsdrome and promoting ice-skating, ballroom dancing and squash courts. The Sportsdrome was entirely destroyed in a bombing raid in 1940, but its replacement, opened in 1952, became one of the city's main sport and entertainment venues.

Charles Knott also had interests in speedway before World War Two at Harringay and Lea Bridge.

Two of Charles Knotts' three sons, Charles Junior and Jack, followed their father into the speedway world. Charles Junior was also a noted Hampshire cricketer, taking 647 wickets for the county with his off-spin and occasional medium pace bowling.

His cricket was often at odds with his business, and sometimes he would have to drive back to Southampton in

The Guv'nor, Charles Knott Senior (far right of photograph), one of the original British speedway promoters and a well-known businessman and personality in his home town of Southampton, celebrates victory in the 1937 Coronation Cup, with his Saints team. (AC)

Southampton were National League champions in 1962 and the era saw many exciting clashes between the top riders of the time, such as this struggle for supremacy between Swedes Ove Fundin of Norwich and home star Bjorn Knutsson. (AC)

the middle of away games in order to deal with a crisis at the fishmonger's or the stadium.

Speedway at Southampton, both in the pre-World War Two era and again during the post-war boom, was in the hands of another veteran promoter, Jimmy Baxter.

The sport's decline brought closure after just a handful of matches in the National League Division Two in 1951, but Charles Knott resurrected the sport for the 1952 season and from that point for more than a decade the Saints were a major part of British speedway, riding at the highest level after Divisions One and Two merged for the 1957 and winning the championship in 1962.

The early 1960s saw the beginning of the property boom in Britain, and the Bannister Court sports complex was situated in a highly desirable part of Southampton.

Speedway promotion, particularly in the days before the large crowds deserted the sport, was primarily a business, albeit one carried on by people with a genuine liking for and interest in the game.

The Knott family received an offer for their Bannister Court assets that was too good to refuse. Happily, their connection with speedway was to continue, and to prove highly beneficial to the sport, along the coast at Poole, where Jack Knott was the key man.

Charles Knott Senior, known throughout the speedway world as 'the Guv'nor' died in 1974, at the age of 83. Charles Knott Junior died in 2003.

The housing estate built on the site of Bannister Court Stadium, next to the cricket ground, was named Charles Knott Gardens, in tribute to both father and son.

Wolverhampton Ladbrokes' Stadium, Monmore Green

The three-storey grandstand at Wolverhampton's Monmore Green Stadium replaced an earlier structure that burned to the ground in the 1960s. The replacement structure and the terracing in front constitutes the only spectator accommodation at Monmore today. (A)

Monmore Green, once an unfashionable and intermittent venue for speedway, is now regarded as one of the jewels in the sport's crown, staging the prestigious British Championship Final.

If speedway racing (and Monmore) are still around in 2028, when the sport in Britain celebrates its centenary, Wolverhampton will have a solid claim to host a commemorative event.

For Monmore Green is the oldest speedway venue still staging the sport in Britain at the time of writing. The stadium opened for greyhound racing on New Year's Day 1928 and some five months later, on 30 May, hosted its first speedway meeting.

The Monmore opener took place almost two months before the first speedway meeting at Belle Vue Greyhound Stadium, Kirkmanshulme Lane – the only other current British venue to have operated in the pioneering season of 1928.

Sadly, if Monmore should survive to stage a British speedway centenary event, there will be virtually nothing left of the original stadium, save the position of the track.

The main grandstand burned to the ground in the 1960s, although the stadium still had sufficient spectator accommodation to allow the then promoter Mike Parker and his right hand man Bill Bridgett to stage a meeting just a few days later.

That couldn't happen today. Although a new and imposing three-tier grandstand was opened in 1969 to replace the old structure, the rest of the spectator accommodation, including covered standing on the back straight and on the fourth bend, has been gradually demolished over recent years.

All that remains, apart from the glass-fronted bars and restaurants in the grandstand, is the very substantial terrace in front of the stand, which is probably capable of holding a couple of thousand spectators.

The permanent terracing has been augmented by temporary stands and altogether fans at Monmore have a good view of the racing, even when the home straight is packed for big meetings such as play-off finals and the British Championship. The grandstand facilities are second to none.

Monmore deserves a look-in at any future commemoration of the sport's history. But unless speedway's following has shrunk to minimal levels by that time, a bigger venue will be needed for the main event.

Monmore Green is also the home of Dudley Heathens, the current incarnation of Cradley Heath. Runners-up in the National League in 2012, attendances for the Heathens matches in the sport's third tier rival those who turn out to watch the Elite League Wolves.

The Heathens' management believes that the crowd levels would increase significantly if the club were to find its own stadium in the Dudley area.

In the meantime, the fierce rivalry that has traditionally existed between the Wolves and the Heathens has been put on hold, for the good of the sport in general.

Start line action from Monmore in 1971 when the spectator facilities, including the stand on the fourth bend and cover on the back straight, were still intact. The tote board advertises greyhound racing at a sister track at nearby Willenhall, in an era when dog tracks were still thick on the ground throughout the West Midlands and the country as a whole. (BPC)

Chapter Five

THE FOOTBALL GROUNDS
– Stamford Bridge to Sittingbourne

Berwick Shielfield Park

Exeter The County Ground

Halifax The Shay Grounds

Poole Wimborne Road

Edinburgh Old Meadowbank

Glasgow Ashfield

Kent/Sittingbourne Central Park

Workington Derwent Park

MANY COMMENTATORS would say that speedway's relationship with football grounds started at the top and went steadily downhill from that point. It is a claim that sounds harsh, but nevertheless bears scrutiny.

The connection between speedway and such top-level football venues as Wembley's Empire Stadium, the Crystal Palace Exhibition Grounds, London's White City (used for two spells by Queens Park Rangers FC), and Hampden Park in Glasgow was dealt with in an earlier chapter.

Other grounds that have staged football at the highest level have also played host to speedway, but in every case the connection was in the sport's earliest days.

Examples include Linfield's ground at Windsor Park in Belfast, the home of Northern Ireland's international football matches, which staged just one speedway meeting in 1928, and other late 1920s/early 1930s venues such as Celtic Park in Glasgow and Chelsea's home ground at Stamford Bridge in London.

Even taking into account the fact that all of these arenas were considerably less developed than they are today, promoters were setting the bar pretty high. It didn't take long for it to be lowered considerably and in later years speedway has ground shared with football clubs from the lower divisions of the Football League, non-league soccer and sides from the two codes of rugby.

Although racing at Celtic's home ground was confined to 1928, Stamford Bridge operated for five seasons, and the team won the initial Southern League in 1929 and the National Association Trophy (the season's curtain raiser to the National

Leaving aside national stadia such as Wembley, Hampden and Crystal Palace, featured in an earlier chapter, the most prestigious British football grounds to stage speedway were Celtic Park , Glasgow (very briefly), and Chelsea's ground in West London. Stamford Bridge, pictured in its earlier days before the development of additional stands had the traditional drawback of a football ground, from a speedway point of view, ie long, narrow straights, and tight bends. (AC)

League) in the track's final year of 1932. The Bridge provided an early example of an issue that was to rear its head constantly when it came to football grounds, namely the fact that tracks around a playing pitch tend to be long and narrow.

In subsequent years, with the majority of the bigger football grounds either unsuitable for speedway, or with directors unwilling to accommodate the sport at any price, promoters had to search either lower down, or even outside, the Football League.

From 1928 onwards, well into the 1990s, speedway continued to find homes at the grounds of clubs in the lower divisions of the Football League (including Barrow's Holker Street, New Brighton FC, The Shay, Halifax and Bristol Rovers' Eastville Stadium). The Pilot Field, Hastings, Wimborne Road at Poole, Romford's Brooklands and Canterbury City's Kingsmead were among the non-league football grounds used for speedway in the south, whilst Fleetwood's Highbury Stadium and Ashington's Portland Park were among comparable venues in the north of England.

The comparative scarcity of specialist greyhound stadia north of the border meant that the majority of Scotland's speedway venues originated as football grounds, mostly from the lower reaches of the professional game

Examples included Edinburgh's pre-World War Two venue at Marine Gardens, at times home to both Leith Athletic and Edinburgh City FC, at Old Meadowbank (again Leith Athletic), Powderhall (Edinburgh City and Leith) and later Shielfield Park in Berwick, Albion Rovers' home at Coatbridge, Cowdenbeath's Central Park, and St Mirren Park in Paisley.

Old Meadowbank, Edinburgh, was a typical Scottish lower division or junior football ground, with one centrally placed grandstand, high enough above the pitch to give a good view, and fairly primitive open terracing around the rest of the perimeter. (PCC)

Glasgow Tigers' current venue at Ashfield is the home ground of junior football (non-league in England and Wales) side Ashfield, and other Scottish junior football stadia have been used over the years.

In Wales, Newport's original home at Somerton Park generally saw football either in the lower divisions of the Football League or in the non-league sphere, although the County team enjoyed one year in Division Two (now the Championship) in 1946-47.

For most of its history speedway's connection with the oval ball game has centred on the 13-a-side rugby league code. No suggestion has ever emerged that the rugby union authorities at Twickenham and Murrayfield in Edinburgh, for long bastions of amateurism, would have tolerated speedway around their sacred turf although, as illustrated in the preceding chapter, the Welsh Rugby Union (WRU) had no qualms about welcoming greyhound racing as an additional source of revenue at Cardiff Arms Park.

Times have changed, with the British Speedway Grand Prix, unwelcome at the new Wembley, well established at the Millennium Stadium, the modern WRU-owned shrine of Welsh rugby union.

Speedway had early tenancies at rugby union grounds, including Farringdon Park (Preston Grasshoppers RFC), and the Recreation Ground at Tredegar in South Wales,

Speedway has been associated with rugby grounds for most of its existence in the UK, mostly from the 13-a-side rugby league code where, for the most part, spectator facilities were better developed than at rugby union grounds. The only current rugby stadium to stage the sport is Derwent Park at Workington, where the steep terracing on turns one and two provides an ideal view of the speedway. (A)

while the best-known example of a rugby union/speedway share was at Exeter, featured in detail in this chapter.

Rugby League has never boasted a major stadium of its own (apart, perhaps, from Odsal), staging its Challenge Cup Finals at Wembley and its annual play-offs at Old Trafford. Speedway has enjoyed a fair share of tenancy at RL grounds, although most have been just outside the top rank of the northern game's arenas.

In addition to Bradford Odsal and Belle Vue Hyde Road (home in the past to Broughton Rangers and later Belle Vue Rangers), rugby league internationals were played before World War Two at two other grounds which also staged speedway, Cardiff White City and Pontypridd's Taffs Vale Park.

The rugby league/speedway cohabitation list, in addition to Bradford Odsal and Belle Vue includes both The Boulevard (Hull RLFC) and New Craven Park (Hull Kingston Rovers), Doncaster Greyhound Stadium (Doncaster RLFC), Liverpool's Stanley Stadium (Highfield RLFC), Sheffield Owlerton Stadium (Sheffield Eagles RLFC) and a current speedway venue, Derwent Park, Workington.

As in the case of established greyhound stadia, professional football and rugby grounds (as well as Exeter) possessed ready made grandstands and terraces.

Today, some of the most interesting (if not the most up-to-date) stadium architecture can be found in the grandstands and other facilities at Poole, Workington, and Ashfield.

Berwick Shielfield Park

When describing well-kept pitches, sports writers like to describe them as being perfectly manicured. Berwick Rangers' Scottish Third Division football ground at Shielfield Park well merits the description.

The impression the visitor takes away from Shielfield is of a stadium that is lovingly cared-for in every possible aspect, by people who are proud of their link with the football club and, by association at least, with the speedway promotion that shares the venue.

The modern-day main stand, reconstructed from an original structure battered into submission by gales from the nearby North Sea, is kept spotlessly clean and tidy.

The back straight has its original terracing, partly covered, and there is elevated viewing on the third bend, claimed by the club to offer the best viewpoint in speedway. This consists of a grassed areas kept in a condition which would do credit to the lawns at a stately home.

The speedway track, with its safety barrier in the black and gold colours of the Berwick Bandits, is a fast, 368 metre (402-yard) circuit, which in recent times has been awarded the annual Speedway Riders Benevolent Event (the Ben Fund Bonanza) and the FIM British round of the World Under 21 Championship.

Although Berwick Rangers play Scottish football, Shielfield Park is firmly on the English side of the border, in the Tweedmouth district of the town, standing cheek by jowl with a huge maltings.

Berwick Bandits were founder members of the British League Division Two in 1968, promoted by Andrew 'Danny' Taylor, a prosperous Borders farmer who sadly died at the end of the inaugural season. His wife Elizabeth and son Ken took over the running of the track.

The Bandits were evicted from Shielfield in 1980 and, still under the direction of Elizabeth Taylor, a new stadium was created at Berrington Lough, near Ancroft, Northumberland, where the club was based from 1982 to 1986. Other directors came on board and the promoting reins changed hands, with Mrs Taylor dying in 1986.

Speedway returned to Shielfield in 1996. Despite reporting considerable problems with viability in 2012, Berwick continued to operate in 2013 and the management continues to embrace progressive policies.

Shielfield Park, situated in the Tweedmouth area of Berwick upon Tweed, is the home of Berwick Rangers FC, the only club based geographically in England to play in the Scottish league. The main stand at Shielfield was rebuilt after its predecessor had been damaged by gales. Behind the stand is the extensive Tweed Valley Maltings of the long-established Simpsons Malt. (A)

The back straight at Shielfield Park has immaculately maintained concrete terracing, with a substantial roofed area. The grass bank on the third bend is regarded as giving an excellent view. (A)

The main stand at Berwick is a prime viewing spot. Spectators in their comfortable seats follow the progress from the gate of Cameron Heaps, Lubos Tomicek, Ricky Ashworth and Morton Risager. (CP)

The club decided to improve safety at Shielfield following a serious crash involving rider Alex Edberg in June 2011. After researching the various air fences on the market, the decision was taken to acquire a revolutionary polyfoam barrier, seen as the perfect match to the Bandits' needs.

The fact that Shielfield is shared with the football club meant there was just a two hour window for weekly installation of the barrier, precluding the use of a traditional inflatable air fence.

Berwick's chief paramedic Marc Kelly is a huge fan of the polyfoam fence, saying:

> I wish every track would install this type of fence. If it gives us a quiet night we are all thankful. It should prevent a great deal of injuries to these brave young men who entertain us.

Edinburgh
Old Meadowbank

In the 1960s Old Meadowbank, Edinburgh, could claim some of the biggest and most enthusiastic crowds in British speedway. The terraced buildings of Edinburgh's Old Town form the backdrop to the stadium. (PCC)

It used to be a well-known saying that dog never ate dog. In reality, many powerful organisations in the sporting world have no hesitation whatsoever in devouring seemingly weaker and less fashionable rivals.

Self-interest dominates much professional sport and the rulers of one game will gladly sacrifice another activity if it suits their purpose.

Local authorities and the governing bodies of sports as diverse as football, rugby and athletics, to say nothing of greyhound racing, have on several occasions gladly connived at the destruction of speedway clubs in order to advance their own causes.

One of the earliest instances of speedway being dumped to make way for a more fashionable sporting experience came in 1967, when the Edinburgh Monarchs were ordered to quit the Old Meadowbank Stadium to make way for a brand spanking new arena for the 1970 Commonwealth Games.

The Edinburgh Corporation, owners of Old Meadowbank, apparently had no concern for the several thousand of their citizens who formed one of speedway's biggest and most loyal fan followings.

As in the case of the Olympic Stadium built for the London 2012 Olympics, or the re-built Wembley Stadium, or at a lower level the new ground constructed for the Exeter Chiefs rugby union team, the suggestion that provision should be made for speedway resulted in at worst either outright derision or at best an embarrassed silence.

Lower division football clubs are equally at the mercy of the financially-obsessed Premiership. West Ham's decision to seek a move to the Olympic Stadium rides roughshod over the rights of Leyton Orient, established in the area for decades.

Old Meadowbank had staged speedway from 1948 to 1954, and again from 1959 until the axe fell. The venue was a classic lower-division Scottish football stadium, with one relatively small stand and a mixture of open banking and rudimentary terracing on the other three sides.

One of the great advantages of a speedway track in a stadium shared with football, with Old Meadowbank a prime example, was the absence of a greyhound track intervening between the crowd and the action. (PCC)

The relatively primitive facilities failed to dampen the enthusiasm of the Edinburgh support, and the track was almost universally popular among visiting riders and fans. The eviction notice for the Monarchs was obviously a body blow to promoter Ian Hoskins, but the complete indifference of all the authorities concerned to the fate of speedway sent shock waves throughout the entire sport.

The revival of Glasgow Tigers in 1964 had provided Edinburgh with a true local derby, and in retrospect this period must rank as a golden era for Scottish speedway. The destruction of the original Old Meadowbank, and the decision to drive a motorway through Glasgow's White City Stadium, set both the Monarchs and the Tigers off on a nomadic chase around a surprisingly large number of venues of varying degrees of quality, which in the case of the Monarchs may not be over, more than four decades on.

Exeter The County Ground

You don't have to look very hard to find a speedway promoter from the past who still has a sizeable bee in his bonnet about far-from-perfect relationships with greyhound managements.

To be fair, the tension between speedway and the owners of the stadia which hosted the sport was by no means confined to the greyhound arenas. Speedway has always contributed plenty of revenue to its hosts, not only through the rental paid to hire the track, but also through the income generated for a venue's restaurants, cafés and bars.

This has generally been retained by the host organisation, and the cash flow in the days when speedway crowds were numbered in the thousands can easily be imagined. In some cases gratitude was in short supply.

One example where the hosts made it perfectly plain that speedway was tolerated purely because of the income it contributed concerned the County Ground at Exeter, one of the sport's oldest and most respected provincial tracks.

Speedway made its bow in the capital of the West Country in 1929. The ground was owned by the Exeter Chiefs Rugby Union Club, and the pitch was surrounded by an asphalt cycle track, which was easily converted into a 400-yard plus speedway circuit.

League speedway arrived in 1947, after the stadium had been vacated by the armed forces, who had occupied it during World War Two. It was at this stage that the previous

The notorious grandstand at Exeter's County Ground home. The facility was extended at the front and extra rows of seats were installed by the landlords, Exeter Rugby Club, without any consultation with the speedway promoters. The changes made it impossible for many spectators watching speedway from the stand to see action on the home straight without standing up. (IHC)

wooden safety barrier was replaced by the steel fence which, allied to the narrow and steeply-banked track, gave the Falcons team a distinct home advantage.

Visiting riders invariably treated the circuit, and the barrier in particular, with considerable respect, although Cornish rider Chris Blewett is reputed to have ridden wall-of-death style on the fence, leaving tyre marks behind.

Respect is not always a word that can be used with regard to the relationship between the rugby union hosts and the speedway promotion.

Exeter were part of the British speedway scene from 1947 for nearly sixty years, and for most of that period, the speedway income was vital to the rugby club. At one stage it was estimated that nine out of ten spectators who passed through the County Ground turnstiles were entering to see the bikes in action.

With rugby union's adoption of professionalism, the Exeter Chiefs began to play a more prominent part in the 15-a-side game. Ambitious to progress to the code's full-time top tier, the club sold the County Ground for development and moved to a new stadium on the outskirts of the city, close to the M5 motorway.

With the rugby club now generating an income undreamed of during most of its history, speedway could be safely put to the sword. There was no space for speedway at the new ground, and you could probably hear the sighs of relief from some of the rugger chaps.

Difficulties with the rugby club were nothing new. In the pre-league, pre-professionalism days, the major rugby games at the County Ground came when the

Residents living next to the back straight at the County Ground had a grandstand view from their bedroom windows. Now the entire stadium is a housing development. (IHC)

This view along the back straight terracing at Exeter shows the narrow track, the banked bends, and the fearsome steel safety fence, hated by many riders (IHC)

South West region was allocated a match against one of the southern hemisphere touring teams.

On one such an occasion the Exeter Chiefs not surprisingly sensed a bumper pay day, and set about some alterations to the stadium to maximise the attendance and the receipts.

The grandstand on the speedway home straight, virtually the only substantial spectator facility available in addition to some concrete terracing below the stand and on the back straight, saw substantial alterations, involving the re-positioning of the seats and the addition at the front of extra rows.

An atmospheric image of the start line and grandstand at the County Ground, Exeter, with a packed crowd enjoying a West Country derby against Bristol. (AC)

The problem was that the hosts had failed to consult speedway promoters Wally Mawdsley and Pete Lansdale about the changes. When the next speedway season began patrons, many of them long-standing season ticket holders, found that their view of the action on the home straight had been blocked by the extension to the front of the stand.

The rugby club was unapologetic. The income from speedway was still rolling in, from Exeter's substantial support.

I have a soft spot for Exeter and the County Ground, as it was the place where I saw my first speedway meeting, back in 1962. On that occasion, and on subsequent visits, I watched the racing from the terrace below the grandstand, or from the back straight.

It took a much later visit, with a young child present, to tempt me up into the grandstand. The truth did not dawn until the riders came round from the pits to the start line, disappearing from view. The evening became a constant case of standing up for the racing and only sitting down to mark the programme.

Speedway has vanished from one of its most distinctive homes, to the great loss of the South West's most attractive city, and despite the great efforts of those with an ambition to bring the sport back again.

Glasgow Saracen Park

No other club can match Glasgow Tigers as speedway's indisputable nomads (although their fierce rivals the Edinburgh Monarchs run them reasonably close).

White City Stadium, Hampden Park, Coatbridge, two venues in Blantyre, a temporary spell at Workington, and Shawfield Stadium – the list is extensive and the category of venue extremely varied.

Ironically, the Tigers' latest (and hopefully their long-term) base, at Ashfield AFC's Saracen Park Stadium, was formerly the venue for another set of rivals, this time from within their own city.

The grandstand and the covered enclosure at Saracen Park, now shared by landlords Ashfield AFC and Glasgow Tigers. From 1949 to 1952 the stadium was the home of Glasgow rivals to the Tigers, the Ashfield Giants speedway team, promoted by Johnnie Hoskins. (A)

Ashfield Giants operated at the Scottish junior football club's base from 1949 to 1952, with some open licence meetings in 1953. During the Giants' years in the National League Division Two, the venue hosted local derbies which for the most part were effectively internecine warfare between the McHoskins tribe.

Scottish speedway in the immediate post-World War Two era was a Hoskins family fiefdom. Johnnie revived Glasgow Tigers at White City in 1946, putting eldest son Ian, then still short of his 22nd birthday and newly released from the RAF, at the helm.

Johnnie was also the motive power behind the introduction of speedway to Old Meadowbank in Edinburgh two years and then created the Giants at Ashfield, spawning talent such as tragic Australian Ken le Breton and is compatriots Merv Harding and Keith Gurtner.

Many reasons have been advanced over the years for the closure of speedway tracks. Two of these apply to Ashfield, one relatively commonplace within the sport, and one probably unique in its circumstances.

The death of le Breton in a crash during a Sydney test match in 1951 was a huge blow to the Giants, just as the accident that claimed the life of Alan Hunt in South Africa in 1957 was cited as one of the reasons for the closure of Birmingham.

The second blow to Ashfield was dealt not by the Grim Reaper but by the dead hand of bureaucracy in the shape of Glasgow Corporation.

Speedway at Ashfield attracted sizeable crowds, at least for local derbies with the other Scottish sides, and this did not escape the notice of Glasgow Corporation.

At a time when the terraces at some large English football grounds consisted mainly of cinders and flimsy cement risers, the Glasgow city fathers ordered Johnnie Hoskins to construct ten rows of high quality concrete terracing, a demand which cost thousands of pounds to put into effect.

Although Hoskins and the Giants team manager, pioneer rider Norrie Isbister, rolled up their sleeves to help with the work, the cost was still crippling. With crowds dipping across the sport in general, the council edict undoubtedly punched a major hole in Ashfield's financial viability.

The terracing on the bends and the back straight at Ashfield, for the most part, is still visible today, although in places overgrown. Greyhound racing was introduced at Saracen Park during the years when speedway was absent from the stadium, but the dog track has given way to speedway again and the

Johnnie Hoskins was forced by Glasgow Corporation to spend thousands of pounds on terracing for Saracen Park, much of which exists today, as pictured on the back straight and the third bend. It was claimed that the expense contributed to the eventual closure of the Ashfield Giants. Considerable track work in recent times improved the spectacle of racing but brought financial problems for the Tigers' management. (A)

The terracing in the covered enclosure at Ashfield gives an excellent and sheltered view of racing. (A)

large totalisator board situated going into bend three is now basically an advertising hoarding.

Saracen Park is one of the speedway venues where spectators are allowed to stand all around the arena and it could be argued that the facilities which cost Johnnie Hoskins so dear are still putting something back into Scottish speedway…

Halifax The Shay Grounds

Halifax is one of a select number of towns and cities where it can be fairly claimed that speedway in its heyday really challenged football and rugby in popularity.

The adherents of both the round and oval ball have had their moments of glory in the former woollen manufacturing centre in West Yorkshire.

Halifax RLFC's honours board records victories in both the Rugby League Championship and the Challenge Cup and the club's historic ground at Thrum Hall saw its record crowd in 1959, when more than 29,000 spectators turned out for a match against Wigan.

Halifax Town Football Club, which in all its Football League career failed to rise above the Third Division (today's League One) nevertheless once attracted a crowd not far short of 40,000 people – or about half the population of the town.

Thrum Hall was also home to a cricket ground, which hosted a handful of Yorkshire county championship matches and also staged speedway in the 1928–1930 period, with the Halifax team finishing third in the English Dirt-track league in 1929.

League speedway returned to Halifax in 1949, with the Dukes team competing in the National League Division Three at the football ground. Promotion to Division Two came the following season, but falling crowds brought about withdrawal at the end of the 1951 campaign.

When speedway operated at The Shay, Halifax in the immediate post-World War Two period, and when the sport was revived at the stadium in 1965, the nominal capacity was very considerable. However, as the top right hand part of the photograph shows, much of the accommodation consisted of cinder banking, albeit with crush barriers, rather than concrete terracing. (AFC)

Halifax, like many other tracks over the years, was unable to retain what had been a high level of initial support. Although attendances peaked at a reported 18,000 in the first season, the average had fallen to fewer than 5,000 by the time of withdrawal.

In the early 1960s the Middlesbrough team was led by a native of Halifax, Eric Boothroyd, who still lived in the town and ran a flourishing greengrocery business. Boothroyd's mechanic, Arthur Ambler, worked for a motor dealer on Skircoat Road, Halifax, close to The Shay and regularly badgered the Bears promoter Reg Fearman to consider returning speedway to West Yorkshire.

Fearman eventually agreed to stop off in Halifax en-route to Teesside, and he and Ambler peered through cracks in the fencing at the ground. Reg Fearman was impressed with the possibilities and although he was at first rebuffed by the football club, the appointment of a new chairman opened the doors to a speedway revival, which became a reality in 1965.

On this occasion the Dukes made a huge impact, both on and off the track, winning the British League title in only the club's second season, and attracting large crowds to The Shay, at a time when both soccer and rugby league was in decline in the town.

Speedway continued at Halifax for two decades, until the promotion team which had succeeded Reg Fearman and Eric Boothroyd transferred the licence to nearby Bradford.

Continued decline for both the football and rugby clubs – Halifax RLFC lost its place in the television era Super League, while Halifax Town were relegated from the Football League and eventually went into administration, being succeeded by a new club, FC Halifax Town – meant the town relied on speedway for its sporting success.

Recent years have seen a revival for both football and rugby league, and the absolute transformation of the ground. Sadly, the squaring off of the two ends and the construction of three new grandstands has ensured that the stadium, now with a 14,000 capacity, can never again be used for speedway.

The Shay in its speedway heyday in the '60s, '70s and '80s could never be described as well-appointed, although there were seats and plenty of cover. On the bends spectators for the most part stood on cinder banks rather than concrete terracing and the mind boggles at the thought of 36,885 people packed into The Shay for a match against Spurs.

In recent years The Shay has been transformed and is now shared by Halifax AFC, no longer members of the Football League, and Halifax Rugby League Club, which sold its old home at Thrum Hall. The stand on the left of the picture is based on the framework of an original facility, and survives, at least for the time being. (AC)

Kent Central Park, Sittingbourne

The story has been beloved of the tabloid newspapers through decade after decade. The larger-than life tales of the big time gambling winners who end up flat broke, disenchanted and struggling to rebuild their often shattered lives.

The main stand at Sittingbourne's Central Park, arguably the most impressive single spectator facility at any British speedway venue, with unimpeded views of the racing and excellent bar and refreshment facilities. Football's loss is a gain for greyhound racing and speedway. (A)

One of the first to make the headlines was football pools first dividend winner Viv Nicholson. She won £152,000 in 1961 (a sum estimated to be worth £5 million in today's values) and famously declared that she would 'spend, spend, spend'. She did, until she had nothing left.

Viv's modern-day equivalents are the lottery winners who scoop millions, start out ecstatic and proclaiming that their lifestyles will not change, yet still wind up broke and in therapy.

This is a modern-day morality tale of a football club which won its own equivalent of the pools or the lottery, wildly overspent, and in the process gifted a superb stadium to greyhound racing and, eventually, to speedway.

Kent has long been a hotbed of non-league football, and many of the clubs and their grounds have from time to time been headline-worthy. Ebbsfleet, formerly known as Gravesend and Northfleet, were pioneers of the supporter co-operative movement, with thousands of fans becoming small-time shareholders in the club.

Johnnie Hoskins turned Canterbury City's ground at Kingsmead, in the shadow of the cathedral, into the speedway arena that gave him an Indian summer.

Then there was Sittingbourne FC. Not one of non-league's bigger or more ambitious names. Or not particularly ambitious until the club sold its ground, a valuable

The back straight at Sittingbourne features an impressive (but roofless) covered terrace. Such facilities are not needed for greyhound racing and currently speedway crowds at Central Park are restricted under normal circumstances to the main stand and terracing on the first and second turns. (A)

property, to a supermarket chain, netting several million pounds from the deal.

Sittingbourne thought big when it came to developing a new stadium. Facilities at the new stadium would include a main grandstand seating 2,500 spectators, an extensive covered terrace on the opposite side of the pitch, and terraced areas behind each goal.

The little Kent football club would, once the work was complete, have one of the best grounds outside the Football League. The problem was that although the supermarket deal had netted £4.5 million in the bank, the club considerably overspent on the construction of the new stadium.

Mr Micawber's advice that having 20 shillings and spending 19s 6d spelt happiness, whilst spending 20s and 6d spelt misery, meant nothing to the football club. Misery was to be Sittingbourne FC's lot.

When Central Park was eventually acquired by a greyhound racing company, the football club was allowed to continue playing at the stadium. This eventually proved beyond the football club's means and it moved to a much more modest ground on an adjacent site. It has been reported that the club intends to leave this arena and ground share with another club.

The greyhounds, and now the speedway, reign supreme at Central Park.

The men behind the new Kent Kings have impeccable speedway pedigrees. Sittingbourne greyhound chief Roger Cearns, grandson of the man who built Wimbledon Stadium, and a former CEO at Plough Lane himself, has joined forces with speedway legend Len Silver.

At the May Day Bank Holiday 2013, Central Park staged its first meeting, attracting more than 3,000 spectators, of which an encouraging number returned for the team's first match in the third tier National League.

The new track faces some formidable obstacles, including a 6.30pm start with an 8.30pm curfew, racing on a Monday evening, against the competition of televised Elite League speedway.

To win planning permission for speedway (a long process), Cearns was obliged to build a special 6 metre (20ft) high acoustic fence at one end of the stadium – a considerable expense to add to the costs of laying down a track, safety fence, pits and all the other equipment needed for the sport.

Kent has in the past been a speedway (and grass-track) hotbed, and few would doubt that if anyone could overcome the obstacles and make a success of Sittingbourne, it is the experienced Cearns and Silver.

This shot of the terracing on the first and second turns at Sittingbourne illustrates the fencing,(6 metres, 20 feet) high, which the promoter was obliged to erect to gain planning consent for speedway. (A)

Poole Wimborne Road

Poole, for the modern-day speedway fan, is the epitome of the model speedway track.

Attendance levels at Wimborne Road are among the healthiest in the game, fired by the success enjoyed by a Pirates' team full of character and which in 2013 boasted both the current World Champion in the form of Australian Chris Holder and a hot tip for a future title holder, in the shape of his fellow countryman Darcy Ward.

Spectator facilities at Wimborne Road are excellent, the club has a progressive and passionate promoter in Matt Ford, and Neil Middleditch is one of the sport's canniest team managers.

Poole Stadium, with the track a hive of activity in the lead-up to a meeting, has both traditional and modern spectator facilities. The open-fronted grandstand, mostly still equipped with the bench seating typical of non-league football grounds, was originally built for Poole Town Football Club. (A)

Above right: Poole's Wimborne Road home, close to the town centre, has all-round viewing. Well-behaved dogs under control are welcome (see bottom right hand corner of the picture). (A)

Right: The modern facility on the back straight at Poole, which replaced a stand constructed in the 1960s, houses restaurants, refreshment facilities, bars and betting facilities for the greyhound crowds. It is also well used for speedway meetings. (AC)

Below: The ground floor interior of the back straight facility at Poole bears more resemblance to a plush airport lounge than a sports stadium, but its comfort is well appreciated by both speedway and greyhound fans. (A)

Yet set against the long record of success at Poole – the Pirates roll of honour includes 13 title wins in various divisions of British speedway since the club was founded in 1948, including four Elite League victories – has been the darker side of life at Wimborne Road.

An unwanted and unprecedented niche in speedway history was ensured virtually from the moment the referee pressed the button to release the starting tapes for the very first time on 26 April 1948.

Reg Craven, riding for the visitors, Yarmouth, was involved in a crash on the first bend of the first lap of the first ever heat at Wimborne Road, sustaining severe head injuries from which he died eight days later. Subsequently, Johnny Thomson (1955) and Malcolm Flood (1956) suffered injuries at the track which led to their deaths.

The stadium dates originally from 1933, and was home to Poole Town Football Club, members of the Western League and subsequently the Southern League.

The traditional open-fronted grandstand, built to seat 1,400 people, was opened in

1961. The facility, which offers an excellent view and is well patronised by the Poole fans, still largely retains the original wooden benches and to this day the riders use the building to change, and then walk across to the pits on the second bend.

When the Knott family from Southampton took over Poole in 1960, a new modern grandstand was constructed on the back straight. This was replaced in 1997 by a glass-fronted facility with dining, bar and viewing facilities, for both speedway and greyhound meetings.

Workington Derwent Park

The immediate post-World War Two period, regarded as a golden age for speedway, also saw the far north-west corner of England enjoy a sporting boom.

Workington Town RLFC, formed in 1944, enjoyed a truly meteoric rise to win the Rugby League Championship in 1951. A year later the club were Championship runners-up but won the sport's Challenge Cup in front of more than 72,000 people at Wembley.

The main grandstand at Workington's Derwent Park, built from brick and steel in the 1950s, was designed with raked ends to allow a perfect view of the rugby league pitch, and has subsequently been a boon to speedway followers. (A)

Heady days for sports fans in the historic Cumberland coal, steel and port town, saw the football team, Workington AFC, gain admission to the Football League in 1951.

Where was speedway in Workington's sporting heyday? Sadly, it had become simply a dim recollection in the memories of older enthusiasts. Although the sport enjoyed a couple of spells of open-licence racing in Workington in the 1930s, a couple of decades later it had completely disappeared from view.

Things were to change dramatically as the 20th century entered its final decades. The rugby league club was unable to maintain its status, and crowds slumped dramatically. During the same era the football club lost its league status, and Workington became a sporting backwater.

The introduction of speedway in 1970 did a great deal to restore sporting morale in what had now become the county of Cumbria.

Today, with the football club still in the doldrums, the sporting order of precedence in Workington ranks speedway and rugby league on more or less the same level, although speedway on average probably pulls in the larger crowds.

Although the rugby league club are the hosts, the sign at the entrance to the Derwent Park venue shared by the two sports sets an encouraging tone, giving equal billing to the rugby outfit and the Comets speedway team.

The pre-World War Two speedway in Cumberland was staged at the home of an earlier rugby league side. Derwent Park was ready for competitive rugby in 1956, with the team moving from a ground share with the football club.

Although the rugby side was never again to reach the heights of 1951-52, there was still a sizeable public for rugby league, with the record attendance at Derwent Park set in 1965 when 17,741 spectators attended a third round Challenge Cup match against Wigan.

Derwent Park was refurbished to stage some group matches in the 2013 Rugby League World Cup. The work included the installation of new seats in the grandstand, which overlooks the speedway start line. (A)

Speedway's Derwent Park debut came in 1970, with the track operating in the British League Division Two and the National League of the period until 1981.

There was a revival on an open licence basis in 1985 and the nomadic Glasgow Tigers used the venue for part of the 1987 season. The team name was switched to Workington Tigers in August, but a month later the team was expelled from the National League. Speedway returned in 1994, with large crowds initially flocking to Derwent Park.

The 2012 season was a difficult one for the Comets, but a take-over by Laura Morgan, in association with her co-promoters, brother Steve Whitehead and Tony Jackson, who also acts as team manager, sparked a major revival.

The new start for speedway has coincided with the refurbishment of Derwent Park, scheduled as the venue for two of Scotland's matches in the 2013 Rugby League World Cup – the reason behind funding for the ground improvements.

The main grandstand at Derwent Park, which gives speedway fans what must rank as one of the finest views of racing in the game, has comfortable new seats. In addition new floodlights and an electronic scoreboard have been added to a stadium which generally looks freshly-painted and well cared-for.

In addition to the grandstand, the venue has covered terracing along the back straight, incorporating a plush hospitality suite, and there is steeply-graded open terracing on turns one and two, where speedway crowds favour the top two or three steps.

The open terracing on the first and second bends at Workington links up with the back straight covered terrace. The enclosed part of the back straight stand is a hospitality suite, with a balcony.

Former fan Laura Morgan and her co-promoters enjoy a good relationship with their rugby league hosts. In addition to some innovative promotion, including making tickets available at a lower price when booked online, the Comets promotion took a gamble on lowering admission prices in general for the 2013 season, and the crowds responded. For Laura, owning the Comets is a dream come true, as she explained:

I'm tremendously proud to be owner of Workington Comets, and launching the club's new era has been a fantastic experience. I have wanted to own this club since I was a little girl, and now my dream is reality.

It's been stressful, and hectic, but there is a lot of adrenaline going through my veins. The team dynamic is superb, and we have been able to overhaul a lot of off-track aspects.

Speedway may have been absent during the heyday of sporting success on the Cumbrian coast but it is now a massively important part of the area's sporting heritage, If there is any justice in the sport's world, Laura Morgan's dedication to the Comets will surely bring more honours to this distinctive part of England.

Chapter Six

PURPOSE-BUILT FOR SPEEDWAY

– Investment Over the Decades

Buxton Hi-Edge Raceway

Coventry Brandon Stadium

Eastbourne Arlington Stadium

Kings Lynn The Norfolk Arena

Mildenhall West Row

Nottingham White City Stadium

Redcar South Tees Motor Sports Park

Scunthorpe Eddie Wright Raceway

Somerset The Oak Tree Arena

Swindon Abbey Stadium

Weymouth Radipole Lane

Cardiff Penarth Road

Cradley Heath Dudley Wood Stadium

Ipswich Foxhall Heath

Leicester Beaumont Park

Norwich The Firs

Plymouth St Boniface Arena

Rye House Hoddesdon Stadium

Sheffield Owlerton Stadium

Stoke Loomer Road

Tamworth The Stadium, Fazeley

SPEEDWAY IN BRITAIN has long been criticised for a perceived collective failure to develop its own venues. The lack of a purpose-built stadium, owned by an organisation with speedway as its raison d'etre and able to stage the biggest events in the sport's calendar has over the years been a constant bugbear for fans and commentators alike.

Given the validity of the claim that speedway has mostly led a cuckoo-like existence, making its home in a nest already built and occupied by other species (usually greyhound racing or football), it comes as something of a surprise that stadia built primarily for the sport easily outnumber venues in the other categories covered by this book.

This is largely because of the decision to include in the work all of the sport's current UK venues, a good proportion of which are purpose-built. Nevertheless, arenas built primarily for

Purpose-built speedway tracks in the modern era need to seek sites acceptable to the planning authorities, in an age when public tolerance of noise, even for two hours a week, is generally low. Redcar's home at the South Tees Motor Park is built on land previously occupied by a steelworks in an area which, as the backdrop shows, is still heavily industrial in nature. (A)

Facilities at speedway's newest stadia are being developed as and when budgets allow. Redcar co-promoter and manager Brian Havelock gives the thumbs up as he stands on the steps of the new grandstand at the South Tees Motor Park. (A)

The Norfolk Arena at Kings Lynn has seen constant investment since the stadium was acquired by the father and son team of Buster and Jonathan Chapman. Investment of a level that would not be possible if the Arena did not also stage a variety of other events. (A)

speedway were certainly not unknown in the sport's early years. Three prime examples constructed in the late 1920s survive to this day, in the form of Coventry's Brandon Stadium, Sheffield's Owlerton Stadium, and Arlington Stadium, Eastbourne.

Other purpose-built venues which still stage the sport today were products of speedway's middle years, the post-World War Two era, when their builders defied the restrictions of the austerity era to find the means to construct a stadium. Ipswich and Swindon belong to this period.

Some purpose-built stadia, from various eras, have fallen by the wayside. These notably include pre-World War Two venues such as the old Olympic Speedway (later the White City Stadium) in Nottingham, and the still much-lamented Firs at Norwich.

Post-war stadia created for speedway which have subsequently vanished include Cradley's Dudley Wood Stadium, Cardiff's short-lived Penarth Road track, and the original Radipole Lane arena at Weymouth.

Kings Lynn's Norfolk Arena, although occupying the site of a 'flapping' greyhound track and one time grass track speedway circuit, was much changed by the time it took its place in the British League in 1966 and has in recent years been utterly transformed.

One of the biggest post-World War Two developments was the creation of Reading's Smallmead Stadium, which opened in 1975, and was a triumph for the vision and tenacity of promoter Reg Fearman.

Allied Presentations, of which Reg was a leading member, had introduced speedway to Reading Greyhound Stadium, Tilehurst, in 1968, as part of the creation of the British League Division Two. The venture was extremely successful, and Reading stepped up into Division One in 1971, winning the British League title in 1973. It was a major shock when it was announced that Tilehurst was to close, leaving the reigning champions homeless.

Fearman refused to accept that this was the end for Reading and masterminded the construction of Smallmead on a former rubbish dump, with racing resuming in the town in 1975. It was a successful venue into the 21st century, but the expiry of the lease led to closure, and hopes of a new stadium for the Berkshire town are fading.

Mildenhall's West Row Stadium, constructed in 1973, was another product of this era, while the steel town of

Scunthorpe has seen no fewer than three venues since the early 1970s. Since the original Saints team was evicted from Quibell Park, a local authority-owned athletics and cycling arena, two new stadia have been constructed in the North Lincolnshire town, with the latest venture, the Eddie Wright Raceway, thriving both on and off the track.

Across the Severn Bridge, Newport saw a new track after the closure and demolition of the Somerton Park football ground. Sadly, with interest in speedway falling well below sustainable levels in Monmouthshire, the new facility at the Hayley Stadium has now fallen a premature victim to the wrecking ball.

Recent years have seen a spate of brand-new speedway venues. Some, like the Oak Tree Arena in Somerset and Hi-Edge, Buxton, have broken new ground for the sport. Others, such as Redcar's South Tees Motor Park, the latest Scunthorpe track, Leicester's Beaumont Park and Plymouth's St Boniface Arena, are essentially welcome replacements for earlier venues.

Over the decades, the sport's purpose-built arenas have varied hugely in terms of the facilities they provide. They include, in Brandon and Owlerton, some of the best stadia speedway has known outside of London, Manchester, and Glasgow.

Other tracks, particularly some of the later ones, have been built on modest budgets, although Leicester's new Beaumont Park is a fine example of how much can be achieved in a short period of time.

Buxton Hi-Edge Raceway

Guy Allott, a speedway rider over three decades and a world-renowned engine tuner since hanging up his leathers, pulls no punches when it comes to describing the track which bears the name of his adopted home town.

'On a pleasant summer day there is really nowhere better to be than Buxton to watch speedway. You have the fresh air and the wonderful scenery of the

The Hi-Edge Raceway at Buxton is the highest speedway circuit in Britain, situated at around 1,800 feet on Axe Edge. The original stadium, now used for stock car and banger racing, is at a higher elevation, to the right of the picture, and when meetings are held simultaneously at the two venues, the car racing spectators watch speedway heats from suitable vantage points. (A)

The view from the pits gate at Buxton's Hi-Edge Raceway, illustrates both the majestic Peak District setting and the grandstand view spectators have from their cars parked on the back straight. (A)

Peak District all around you. But if the weather is not so good, then it is more like cinder hell than cinder heaven. The conditions are something only us barbarians who live up here can cope with.'

Guy, one of the men actively involved in bringing speedway to the area, knows what he is talking about. He has watched hours of racing in all weathers at the Hi-Edge Raceway, particularly when grandson Adam was riding for the Hitmen.

It is nothing new for a speedway venue to be some considerable distance from the city or town whose name it bears. Where the Hi-Edge Raceway differs from other one-step-removed speedway venues, lies in the fact that the distance involved is vertical.

The track is just three miles from the Derbyshire spa town, but whereas Buxton, at 1,000 feet above sea level is already the highest town in England, riders and spectators need to climb for more than another 800 feet on to Axe Edge, a major area of gritstone moorland to the south west of the town, to reach the speedway track.

Once arrived on the moor, the first-time spectator then has to be careful to enter the correct stadium. The speedway track is tucked away behind the club's original venue, which is now used only for stock car racing and other four-wheel events.

Given the altitude and the high average rainfall, it is something of a minor miracle that Buxton survives as a speedway venue. Mind you, sports fans in the area are used to extreme conditions. In June 1975, the County Championship match between Derbyshire and Lancashire at the town's attractive cricket ground was disrupted by snow!

Buxton is speedway at most basic, but is none the worse for that. The track, with its wide bends and well-designed safety fence, offers the young novices who predominate

The home straight at Buxton, showing the referee's box, with the pits in the background. The rocky nature of the surrounding hillsides is evident and scattered around outside the stadium are the remains of depots where bombs and ammunition were stored during the Second World War. (A)

in third-tier (National League) racing the safest possible conditions under which to learn their trade.

The concentration on safety has proved effective. The author has seen a race where all four riders fell on the first bend, but with plenty of space for taking avoiding action, there were no injuries to speak of.

There is no covered accommodation for spectators on Axe Edge, and on many occasions, even at the height of summer, many fans watch from the comfort and warmth of their cars, which can be drawn up around the circuit.

Cardiff's short-lived track at Penarth Road provides a wealth of detail. The track operated for just two and a half seasons in the early 1950s. After closure the stadium remained in a state of dereliction until final redevelopment of the site in 1969. (MKC)

Cardiff Penarth Road

After speedway's initial boom years, when some short-lived venues were very primitive indeed, the sport operated for the rest of the pre-World War Two era almost exclusively in well-appointed stadia.

Because this pattern continued, with very few exceptions, into the 1940s and 1950s, the construction of brand new arenas with only basic facilities, on green field or brown field sites, has tended to be seen as a wholly modern trend.

This ignores the fact that there were examples of new basic stadia built in the immediate post-World War Two period. Although possessing little in the way of creature comforts for spectators, these venues had nevertheless to battle through a great deal of red tape surrounding the extremely strict building regulations of the time, and the widespread shortage of materials.

Cardiff's Penarth Road Stadium (Hedon Stadium, Hull was another example) represented one such triumph for local enthusiasm, in the face of a formidable array of obstacles.

The Welsh capital's pre-World War Two speedway venue, the White City Stadium, closed before the outbreak of hostilities, driven out of business by the introduction of greyhound racing at the city's Arms Park rugby stadium, in the heart of the city (see page 54).

Nevertheless, the post-war speedway boom encouraged local businessmen Major A. J. Lennox and Leslie Maidment to construct a completely new circuit at Penarth Road. The low-level aerial shot of the stadium, issued as a postcard at the time, provides an almost-perfect snapshot of the venue.

Although the stadium was basic, it contained most of the facilities necessary to enjoy a meeting, with the exception of covered accommodation, a major omission in an area with more than its fair share of rainfall.

The sizeable nissen hut on the back straight, in front of the railway embankment, is the centrepiece of the pits area, and there is ample evidence around the circuit of other low key or temporary buildings housing turnstiles and refreshment facilities.

The spectators are accommodated in either open temporary stands on either side of the elevated referee and commentary box on the start line, underneath which was the only cover in the entire stadium.

These stands appear to have bench-type seating, but apart from that the only alternative for supporters was to stand on the earth and cinder banking constructed around the rest of the circuit.

The Cardiff promoters were a little slow to get off the mark, with the track making its competitive debut in 1951, just as the post-war boom in speedway's popularity was beginning its severe decline.

At first, it didn't seem to matter that elsewhere in the sport enthusiasm was starting to wane. Cardiff Dragons took their place in the National League Division Three and despite only a moderate position in the table, the crowds rolled in, reportedly up to 20,000 at a time.

In 1952, the same year that Ipswich, another brand new built-for-speedway track opened to big crowds, the Dragons finished runners-up to Rayleigh in the division (now renamed as the Southern League). Buoyed by this enthusiasm, the Cardiff supporters argued vehemently for promotion to Division Two.

When it became apparent that the team was to remain in the third tier, there was widespread resentment among the supporters. This may have been a substantial factor in an almost overnight collapse of support, midway through the track's final season of 1953.

Penarth Road had nothing to sustain its continued existence once the speedway had folded. The venue had been used in the winter of 1951-52 by Cardiff Rugby League Club, who had gained admittance to the Rugby Football League, but this venture, like other attempts to establish the 13-a-side game in the city, was short-lived.

The decaying infrastructure of the Penarth Road Stadium lingered on until demolition for redevelopment in 1969, with no apparent attempt to revive speedway in all those years of disuse.

It was reported at the time of closure that the Cardiff promotion had seen an average crowd of 9,000 in 1952 slump to a third of that figure at the time of withdrawal.

The fact that speedway as a whole endured a difficult summer in 1953, with the massive jump in television ownership triggered by the Coronation of Queen Elizabeth II, allied to a wet summer, was another factor in the ultimate failure of Cardiff's second track.

But the huge decline in interest following massive initial enthusiasm – the Dragons had 12 branches of the supporters club across South Wales in 1952 and British Railways offered cheap tickets on speedway nights to the nearby Grangetown station –is symptomatic of the fact that speedway has proved in the past in many areas that it can at first draw impressive crowds, but then fail to sustain interest.

Coventry Brandon Stadium

Brandon, in these uncertain times for speedway, can perhaps be best compared to an old and particularly well-loved relative, considered to be in shaky health and likely to expire at any time.

There are two current schools of thought about the future of what is arguably the finest regular speedway venue in the UK today, albeit one that seems to have fallen out of favour with the British Speedway Promoters Association (BSPA) when it comes to the allocation of major meetings.

The fact that the venue was owned by Midland Sports Stadiums allowed major investment at Coventry's Brandon Stadium in the final quarter of the 20th century. The new stand at Brandon, with its outdoor seating curving round the first bend, represents perhaps the sport's most important infrastructure investment in that or any later period, apart from the development of completely new stadia. (RH)

If you are naturally a pessimist, you tend to believe that Brandon is living on borrowed time, and will ultimately suffer the same fate as other re-developed Midlands stadia. Young families, they say, will eventually be making their homes on Boocock Road and Olsen Avenue.

Optimists point to the considerable level of investment at Brandon under its current ownership, the revival (once again) of greyhound racing at the stadium, and the likelihood that the local council will continue to oppose the replacement of a sports facility by yet more housing.

Many hearts (including my own) missed a beat a couple of seasons ago with the stand-off between the Bees' management and the BSPA, with the temporary exclusion of the club from the Elite League.

No-one outside the inner circle of speedway could be completely confident that common sense would eventually prevail and that Coventry (and Peterborough, also on the outside for a time) would come to the tapes when the season started.

Most people found it difficult to imagine British speedway without Coventry, a permanent presence in the sport for nearly seven decades. Yet no doubt people said the same thing about New Cross, Wembley, Norwich and Southampton.

By speedway's admittedly rather low standards, Brandon is a fine stadium.

Coventry's back straight also affords covered accommodation. Brandon has always managed to maintain a good track surface whilst at the same time staging well-attended stock car racing, providing a vital income stream. Greyhound racing, first staged at Brandon in 1978, ceased in 2009 but resumed in 2012. (RH)

The old wooden grandstand at Brandon, pictured from the apex of the first and second bends. The local newspaper, now the *Coventry Telegraph*, has always given good coverage to speedway, including special Saturday evening wrap-around editions. (CP)

The magnificent grandstand along much of the home straight, curving around part of the first bend, is a rare instance of a company investing heavily in an existing arena, during the sport's prosperous era in the late 1960s and 1970s.

The transformation of Brandon was not without its controversial aspects, with some disgruntled fans contending over the years that the work was paid for by the sale of Midland Sports Stadiums' other assets.

Be that as it may, those who knew Brandon before the construction of the new facilities, could only hail a huge improvement.

Away from the grandstand, all of Brandon is terraced (although the steps are crumbling in places) in a manner once commonplace at speedway's major stadia. It is a basic aid to comfortable viewing rare elsewhere, in a domestic speedway scene where far too many venues have seen spectator accommodation cut back to the bare minimum

There is adequate cover for popular side patrons, good dining and hospitality facilities, bars and plenty of fast food outlets, while one of the crowning glories is a viewing area looking directly down into the pits – another facility sadly lacking at venues where the fans are denied any sight of the riders making their preparations for racing.

Personally, I have decided to plump for the optimists' camp, and look forward to annually renewing my acquaintance with Brandon. I hope Midland fans will continue to heed the slogan coined by promoter *par excellence* Charles Ochiltree. when he urged supporters to 'Make it a Date by Brandon Gate'.

Cradley Heath Dudley Wood Stadium

A visit to Cradley Heath was a tasty treat indeed for speedway fans, whichever team attracted their main allegiance. Dudley Wood generated an atmosphere arguably unmatched by any other venue in the country.

It was truly an experience to be savoured, just as much as the taste of traditional Black Country fare like faggots and peas, and mild beer from cherished local breweries like Bathams, Holdens and Banks.

Dudley Wood Stadium, Cradley Heath, with the referee's box perched precariously on stilts in front of the covered stand on the home straight. (BAC)

You were guaranteed to find it completely satisfying. That is, of course, if you could find the stadium in the first place.

The Black Country was and is a complex tangle of small towns. Each has a distinct character, but for the visitor the boundaries between each district can be

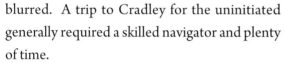

blurred. A trip to Cradley for the uninitiated generally required a skilled navigator and plenty of time.

As a native of the area might say, 'Wier am yow?'

Peter Wrathall, who rode for the Heathens in the 1960s, confesses to having approached Dudley Wood for his first six home meetings by six different routes. The adventure of returning to his South Derbyshire home in the dark, after the crowds had gone home, is another story altogether.

Of course, every speedway track that vanishes from the fixture list is sadly missed by its diehard fans. It is safe to say that Cradley Heath is missed by the sport as a whole. At least today the area has a team, in the shape of the Dudley Heathens, and hopefully a new track in the borough itself will soon be forthcoming.

The support for Dudley Heathen's matches at Monmore Green, Wolverhampton, home of Cradley's traditional and deadly rivals, suggests there is still an eager public.

The story of the fight to try and prevent the closure and redevelopment of Dudley Wood is well known, but struggle was nothing new where the stadium was concerned. Local people had to display considerable patience and determination decades before, when their bid to establish a speedway track was frustrated by both red tape and the intervention of World War Two.

Sports lovers in Cradley Heath applied to the local council for permission to develop a stadium as early as 1936, but it took three years of wrangling before this was forthcoming. Work began to clear a derelict fairground site at the rear of the Victoria public house in Dudley Wood Road, but the declaration of war brought this to an end.

After the war the local authority responded more swiftly to pleas for a speedway track and the local men responsible for the 1930s initiative joined forces with Birmingham businessmen to promote the sport and construct a stadium. The necessary expertise to actually run the speedway came from Les Marshall, promoter at Birmingham.

The first speedway meeting was staged in June 1947. Cradley were founder members of the new National League Division Three, and opened with a win over Wombwell. The Colliers were suitable opponents, coming from a close-knit and distinctive South Yorkshire coal and steel environment not that far removed in spirit from the Black Country.

Cradley was badly hit by the decline of the sport in the early 1950s and, no doubt to

Above left: The subject of track covers to help save meetings from being postponed in wet conditions is much talked about today, The track at Cradley Heath's Dudley Wood Stadium, pictured looking towards the pits on the third bend, is completely covered by tarpaulins in this late 1960s shot. (BAC)

Looking from the home straight to the terracing on the back straight at Dudley Wood Stadium, Cradley Heath. (BAC)

Dudley Wood was notable in the 1960s and early 1970s for having a number of aircraft nose cones in the pits, which afforded some shelter to the riders in bad weather. Pictured in front of one of the cones are, left to right, Ralph Tromans, Bob Andrews, Cradley Supporters Club secretary Irene Prichard and Bernt Persson (on the machine). The little boy is Ralph Tromans's son. (BAC)

the horror of local fans, 'amalgamated' with Wolverhampton for the 1953 season. The track was in at the start of speedway's revival six years later, staging a 'pirate' meeting in 1959 and then being a founder member of the Provincial League the following year.

For many years the Heathens enjoyed only modest success on the track, although the crowds continued to flock to Dudley Wood on Saturday evenings.

The team took part in both the first meeting staged by the 'black' Provincial League Promoters Association in 1964 (at Exeter, with the return leg of a challenge match at Cradley a few days later) and again made history by forming the opposition at Coventry in the first-ever British League match in 1965.

The passionate support the Heathens received from the crowd sometimes led to controversy, and more than one opposition rider had to be smuggled out of Dudley Wood after raising the ire of the supporters.

Cradley was one of the tracks where an electric atmosphere was generated despite the surroundings and facilities failing to match up to some of the better-appointed stadia.

In the best Black Country tradition, make-do-and-mend was often the key phrase. At one stage in the 1960s the stadium management introduced aeroplane nose cones into the pits, to provide some rudimentary shelter.

Access to the nose cones was, however, not for everyone. Peter Wrathall remembers that they were reserved strictly for the heat leaders.

After years of failing to pull up many trees, Cradley finally became a phenomenal speedway success story. The team raced at the highest level of British speedway from 1965 until disbanding at the end of 1996, with the final season spent racing at Stoke, following the closure of Dudley Wood.

The Heathens won the British League championship title twice in the 1980s, and enjoyed eight successes between 1979 and 1989 in the Knock-out Cup. Seven speedway individual World Championships were won by Cradley riders between 1981 and 1996 – three for Erik Gundersen, two for Bruce Penhall and one each for Jan O. Pedersen and Billy Hamill. In addition, former Heathen Greg Hancock won the World title under the Grand Prix system in 1997 and again in 2011, while Anders Michanek, World Champion in 1974, appeared in Cradley colours in 1977.

Eastbourne Arlington Stadium

Many sports arenas are impossible to separate from the personalities who made them famous, with Brian Clough at Nottingham Forest and Dennis Compton at Lords prime examples.

Eastbourne's Arlington Stadium is indelibly associated with not just one individual but with four generations (to date) of the Dugard family.

When I visited Arlington the first person I met was a friendly and efficient young man issuing car park tickets. When I located the pits, the same young man was placing into position tool chests almost as big as himself.

He disappeared from view, but returned a few minutes later wheeling a speedway machine into its allocated spot. The name on the mudguard provided an explanation: Kelsey Dugard, son of former Eagles star Martin, grandson of senior promoter Bob and great-grandson of dynasty founder Charlie.

With his brother Connor also competing, the survival of the Dugard connection seems assured. Just a few days after our meeting, Kelsey took fourth place in the 500cc class in the second round of the British Youth Championship at Rye House, and is hopeful of a team birth with Kent Kings in the National League.

There must have been times in the past when Arlington's relative remoteness – the stadium is several miles from the South Coast seaside resort whose name the team bears – must have seemed like a disadvantage.

Eastbourne, once a fairly primitive Sunday afternoon track, has been extensively developed in recent years and the Eagles are now respected members (and former champions of) the Elite League. The main grandstand has a clubroom and bar above the open seating area. (A)

Arlington Stadium has retained its attractive woodland setting, some miles from the seaside resort whose name the speedway team carries. The entrance to the pits is bustling with activity in this shot, all in view of grandstand patrons and the crowd on the first and second bend terracing. (A)

In the days when many speedway fans lacked their own cars, the trek out to Arlington by public transport required real dedication.

Today, the location, isolated among woodland far from sizeable residential areas, is a major advantage considering the problems other venues have faced from anti-noise protestors.

For decades Arlington was essentially a training track, a Sunday afternoon venue for open meetings and Southern Area League speedway. Eastbourne's first venture into league speedway, in the National League Division Three in 1947, was a huge success on track, with the team winning the league championship.

It was not, however, financially rewarding for promoter Charlie Dugard, who moved the team along the Sussex coast to Hastings, where the operation thrived until forced out of business by residents' claims about noise.

It was an ironic ending to the episode, given that noise was perhaps the least of Dugard's concerns at Arlington.

Photographs from the 1950s, when the stadium had already been in existence for some thirty years, reveals its essentially primitive nature, with spectators standing amongst the trees beside a rudimentary safety fence.

Since that time, Arlington has been transformed by the Dugard family. A seated stand with a clubroom/bar above, a covered terrace on the home straight, extensive terracing on the first and second bends, excellent pits, an electronic scoreboard and good refreshment facilities make a visit to the circuit a pleasant experience, particularly on a balmy summer evening.

This shot of the home straight at Arlington shows the extensive covered terracing and the distinctive control tower at the start line. (A)

As at Kings Lynn and elsewhere, the hard surface stock car track at Arlington sits between spectators and the speedway circuit. But stock cars and other short-circuit car racing classes attract significant crowds to the stadium, and no doubt play a part in helping to keep speedway alive.

Tradition still plays a part in Arlington's presentation. Although presentation generally is up-to-the-minute, speedway nights still begin with a rousing rendition of the county's own anthem, *Sussex by the Sea*.

Ipswich Foxhall Heath

The very name of the traditional home of the Ipswich Witches is redolent of a lonely and blasted heathland location, where flying broomsticks and the black arts would seem just as much at home as flying shale.

The first surprise for the newcomer is how close the stadium actually is to the Suffolk town. And although the stadium's owners (the Spedeworth stock car organisation) have only recently begun to re-develop many of the arena's facilities, the over-riding impression gained by the first-time visitor is of a big, impressive and atmospheric bowl.

Ipswich's introduction to speedway came towards the tail-end of the great post World War Two boom. Although there had been moves to introduce the sport in the late 1940s, and there was open licence activity in 1950 and 1951, Ipswich did not gain admission to the sport's third tier league, by now named the Southern League, until 1952.

Although attendances across the country had started to dip steeply by this time, no-one had told the Suffolk public, and speedway magazines of the time show photographic

A panoramic view of Foxhall Heath, the home of Ipswich Speedway since the early 1950s. Taken from the terracing on the first and second bend, the photograph shows the small grandstand on the home straight, the hard surface stock car circuit, and the vast new open stand at the end of the back straight, erected by the stock car promoting company, Spedeworth, which owns the stadium and is carrying out a programme of improvements. (A)

evidence of the size of the crowds that flocked to Foxhall's substantial terraces.

Although the shrinking shape of speedway meant Ipswich soon found themselves in the National League Division Two, and eventually in the single division formed out of the sport's surviving tracks in 1957, enthusiasm waned at Foxhall.

For a decade or so speedway at the track was intermittent, taking in a spell in the Southern Area League, followed by a return to the top flight which was terminated by a mid-season closure in 1962.

John Pilblad, that indefatigable champion of speedway's apparent lost causes, ran open meetings and fixtures in the short-lived Metropolitan League in the mid-1960s, but the next significant development had to wait until and evening in 1969 when wannabe promoters John Berry and Joe Thurley, both sadly now deceased, climbed over a fence to view an empty stadium.

Berry and Thurley found that the original 410-yard shale track had been covered in tarmac for stock car racing. They were not disconcerted, and laid a 328-yard speedway circuit inside the stox track. Starting off in the British League Division Two, Berry and Thurley laid the foundations for one of the sport's biggest success stories of the last quarter of the 20th century.

On a cool April evening at Foxhall Heath, there are nevertheless a few takers for the open stand and the panoramic view it offers of the racing. (A)

The Witches were British League champions in 1975, 1976, 1984 and 1998, and also won the knock-out cup on seven occasions. The team's successes were spearheaded by local discovery John Louis, whose status as a local hero was later to be taken up by his son Chris, a Grand Prix rider until his retirement and now a respected TV commentator.

Today John Louis is promoter at Foxhall Heath with Chris as Director of Speedway.

Although the Witches stepped down from the Elite League in 2010 to regroup, support at Foxhall remains enthusiastic and loyal. Placing a speedway track within a tarmac stock car circuit is not the ideal situation for bike fans, and in my opinion at least was a disastrous failure at Wimbledon.

It somehow seems to work at Foxhall, and with a huge new grandstand of the type perhaps more commonly seen at major golf tournaments situated at one end of the back straight, together with re-developed hospitality facilities and other amenities, the stadium's owners cannot be faulted.

Work is also taking place progressively to improve the extensive, but in some places crumbling, Foxhall terracing.

There is little doubt that a return to the top tier of speedway will eventually put one of the sport's most iconic venues back in the big time.

Kings Lynn The Norfolk Arena

One of the favourite complaints of those speedway followers who like to air their real or imagined grievances on web forums has been the sport's lack of investment in spectator facilities.

They have obviously not been anywhere near Kings Lynn's Norfolk Arena in recent years.

The transformation by the father and son duo of Buster and Jonathan Chapman, of what had once been a fine, FIM- approved venue, but had subsequently deterioriated badly, is quite simply breathtaking.

Although the website whingers prefer to close their eyes to the developments at Kings Lynn, the Stars fans to whom I chatted when I spent an evening at the Norfolk Arena have no doubts whatsoever about the turn-around at the track over the last decade or so.

The present-day status of the venue is obvious from the moment you drive into the car park and see the neat new buildings that surround the circuit.

Admission is via the box office, where state-of-the-art touch-screen machines provide the same sort of tickets provided for the Grand Prix crowds at Cardiff. Next to the box office, and open daily to provide an extra source of revenue for the promotion is the Pit Stop Café.

Once through the gates the first thing to catch my eye was a sign on newly-erected steelwork promising a new seated grandstand. The development at the Norfolk Arena is continuous, as Jonathan Chapman explained.

> When we bought the stadium it had been declared unfit for purpose, and Kings Lynn lost its speedway for a year. Since that time we have spent about £1.5 million over a ten-year period, and we invest between £100,000 and £200,000 every close season.
>
> A lot of the development is obvious, in the form of the new stands and other facilities, but quite a lot of the money we spend goes on the things that are not always immediately obvious to the fans, like concreting, but all contribute to making the place clean, tidy and safe.

To anyone with substantial experience of sports stadia, it is obvious that a good deal of thought as well as cash has gone into the development of the Norfolk Arena.

The covered standing areas close to the start line on the home straight and the facility which extends along the whole of the back straight are both well-protected from the winds which are not uncommon in this flat, fenland area.

Inside the covered areas, and on the open areas on the bends (the entire stadium is terraced), the steps have been made high enough to ensure that everyone gets a good view.

The uncovered seating stand, located at the entrance to the first bend and

The open stand at the
Norfolk Arena,
strategically positioned
where the home straight
meets the first bend, was
in the process of being
doubled in size during
the early spring of 2013,
as part of the continuing
investment in the
stadium by owners
Buster and Jonathan
Chapman. (A)

The whole of the back
straight at the Norfolk
Arena has covered
terracing, well protected
against inclement
weather, and with
plenty of refreshment
facilities. (A)

The fans view from the
stand on the home
straight at the Norfolk
Arena, looking towards
the first and second
bends. (A)

overlooking the pits, was at the time of my visit being extended back towards the start line. The facility towers above the track, giving an uninterrupted view and was well-populated even on a fairly chilly spring evening.

The all-day opening of the Pit Stop Café gives a clue to the philosophy behind the Chapman management of the Norfolk Arena. The place has to earn its living on far more than one speedway night a week.

A key advantage possessed by the Chapmans is the fact that they are among the tiny minority of speedway promoters who actually own the stadium where the team races. Activities at the Norfolk Arena are fully in their hands and they are not dependent upon the whims of others.

Although both Buster and Jonathan regard themselves primarily as speedway people, they are emphatic that the shale sport alone could not have funded the investment at the stadium.

The Norfolk Arena also stages stock cars and bangers, and is home to concerts and other events. Roadside posters visible en-route to Saddlebow Road also announce Robin Reliant racing, proving that any event that turns a profit is welcome at the venue.

Being in full control of the stadium means that, unlike at other venues, the effect upon the track surface of stock cars and bangers can be factored in efficiently to the maintenance of the circuit.

Jonathan Chapman is clear where the business stands.

Although we are speedway people, we are in the entertainment industry. Everything we stage at the Norfolk Arena helps to both maintain and develop a stadium which in recent years has seen top speedway events including World Cup racing. Our aim is to continue to provide the best facilities, not only for our loyal speedway fans but for everyone who comes through our turnstiles.

Leicester Beaumont Park

It has been proven pretty conclusively in recent years that all you really need to successfully promote speedway racing is a track, safety fence, lighting, pits, a fence to prevent fans getting in free of charge, toilets and a bar/clubhouse/burger van.

Opening night at Leicester's new Beaumont Park home, seen from a vantage point above turn one, with the pits just out of sight on the right. Clearly visible are the two temporary stands on the start line and the permanent covered terrace on the back straight. (SD)

A panoramic view of Beaumont Park seen from the pits, with the stadium complete and ready to open.(SD)

Above right: A close-up of the substantial temporary stands flanking the race control centre at Beaumont Park. (SD)

Speedway's 21st century hard core of support (and in some cases they have to be pretty hardy individuals) have demonstrated that they will turn out to follow their favourite sport despite the absence of the spectator facilities fans once more or less took for granted at the stadia of the past.

Some of the newer tracks which started off with the most basic of facilities have subsequently provided covered accommodation, while others still lack a roof to put over the head of the crowd.

When David Hemsley created Leicester's new Beaumont Park arena, bringing speedway back to one of its traditional strongholds after an absence of nearly thirty years, he did it in some style.

Seated grandstands either side of the start line, essentially of a temporary design but covered, and a more permanent roofed terrace along the length of the back straight, together with fairly steep banking around the rest of the arena, mean Lions fans can get a good view of their speedway, in a fair degree of comfort, from every part of the stadium.

In fact, the spectator facilities at Beaumont Park , at the time of writing being augmented by the first phase of a permanent pavilion-style building on the home straight, could be said to have been more of a success than the actual track shape, which was substantially altered for the 2013 season following some criticism.

Milenhall, currently operating in the National League, the third tier of British speedway, have a stadium worthy of a higher status. This view looks across the pits area, situated by the first bend, to the covered stand on the home straight. (BL)

Hemsley's instant reward for his vision and investment was a sell-out crowd of some 4,500 on the opening night 2011, and a steady crowd figure ever since.

The Leicester revival is following a well thought-out plan, which will eventually take the club into the Elite League where it undoubtedly belongs.

Mildenhall West Row

Speedway's settings over the years have covered the entire environmental spectrum, from grim inner-city industrial to rural bucolic.

Few, if any, of the venues used by the sport can be quite as rural as Mildenhall.

Getting to West Row involves a longish drive from

the small Suffolk country town which is perhaps best known for the huge military airfield on its fringe. It means driving along seemingly endless straight flat country roads, driven across fen country characterised by black earth and deep roadside ditches ever ready to claim the unwary motorist.

The first time visitor, after a while, begins to wonder whether a speedway track of any kind could possibly exist in such a lonely spot. Then, all of a sudden, the stadium appears, flanked by car parks the size of which reflect the wide horizons of the fens.

The big surprise upon arrival is the quality of the stadium you discover in the middle of nowhere. West Row is a substantial arena, which staged competitive speedway for the first time in 1975 and is now also home to greyhound racing.

The stadium divides roughly half and half into a fully-developed segment and an area still waiting to fulfil its potential.

It represents another laudable example of promoters investing in speedway (and greyhound racing) in a realistic manner.

Mildenhall's West Row Stadium has further covered accommodation and terracing around the first bend. The stadium has extensive catering and bar facilities. (BL)

Norwich The Firs

Almost half a century since The Firs closed its doors for the final time, memories of Norwich's legendary speedway venue continue to burn as brightly as ever in the minds of older fans.

Not that a fascination with The Firs is just the prerogative of older supporters. Just as speedway followers of all ages post comments on websites to the effect that the rider they most regret never having seen in action is Peter Craven, so many of the younger

Packed terraces and car parks at The Firs, Norwich, in 1950. Note the large number of coaches in the top left and top right hand corners of the photograph, which have in some cases brought home fans considerable distances from Norfolk towns and villages, together with away supporters. Bullards Beers, advertised on the grandstand roof, were a staple part of life in Norwich until the brewery sold out to a national firm. (MKC)

generation admit to a deep regret that they never had the chance to watch racing at Norwich.

The surviving images of The Firs, the memory of which is lovingly preserved by Norwich Stars' number one fan and historian Mike Kemp, show a venue which was relatively basic in its facilities, although especially renowned for the standard and friendliness of its clubrooms and their after-meeting gatherings.

The facilities at Norwich were fairly basic in their construction, but the crowds were always large and the atmosphere something to be savoured. (MKC)

Norwich's glamour came from the excellent standard of racing which was the norm at The Firs, and the track's association with riders out of the very top drawer.

Grass speedway was the mainstay at The Firs throughout the early and mid-1930s, but all changed in 1937 when the first superstar name to be associated with Norwich, Australian Max Grosskreutz, was appointed manager and the Stars entered the Provincial League.

Norwich remained in the second tier of league speedway until the outbreak of World War Two, and re-opened immediately after the end of the conflict, taking one of the six places in the 1946 Northern League.

The Stars had rejected promotion to the top tier in 1939, but eventually reached National League Division One in 1952. Although promotion (never automatic) was a major bone of contention within the sport at that time, Norwich's back-to-back Division Two championships in 1950 and 1951 meant that their claim to top rank status could not be ignored.

The Firs in March 1964, at the start of the stadium's last season of existence. (IMKC)

The names of Stars' top men of the 1950s and 1960s – Ove Fundin, Aub Lawson and Olle Nygren – need no introduction to speedway fans of any age. Top up this list with the likes of Cyril Roger, Billy Bales, Trevor Hedge and many more, and the pedigree of

the men who wore the race jacket with a star on the front is obvious.

Norwich's heyday also typified an era in speedway in which loyalty to one track and to its fans mattered far more than it does today, when riders switch countless times in their career.

Ove Fundin's career record, seen simply as a set of statistics, may show that he he rode for (brief) spells at Long Eaton, Belle Vue, and for the revived Wembley Lions in 1970, as well as for clubs in his native Sweden.

Lies, damn lies, and statistics. Fundin did indeed ride elsewhere than at Norwich, but his heart was always at The Firs.

To this day he remains as proud of the fact that he is a Freeman of the City of Norwich (an honour, as he loves to explain, he shares with Admiral Lord Nelson), as he is of any of his long, long list of speedway honours and titles.

Plans have been announced for a possible revival of speedway in the Norfolk city, at Norwich's showground. This would be a huge boost for the sport as a whole, although the ownership of the name 'Stars', acquired by Kings Lynn in the 1960s after the closure of The Firs, might be an issue!

Nottingham White City

Virtually all of the United Kingdom's major cities have at some stage been home to speedway racing since the sport's revival at the end of World War Two.

At one time or another the vast majority of the English regional capitals, from the south west to the north east, have taken their place alongside tracks in the great cities of London, Edinburgh, Glasgow, Cardiff and even (if only briefly) Belfast, on the sport's fixture list.

The White City Stadium, photographed by the late Dick Smart in 1936, showing the main grandstand and the covered terrace on the fourth bend. (DS)

Many of the names that featured in the early league structure, particularly in the north of England, representing in the main medium-sized urban centres like Barnsley, Rochdale, Warrington, Burnley, and others, were effectively long defunct before the outbreak of hostilities in 1939.

That criteria certainly did not apply to the two greatest exceptions to the general rule. Nottingham and Leeds are among the top ten cities (and the most renowned sporting centres) in England but last staged league racing, at second tier level, in 1937 and 1938 respectively.

In the mid-to-late 1940s, when existing and would-be promoters were criss-crossing the land in order to find suitable venues for a booming sport, it would have been natural for Nottingham and Leeds to have topped the list of their targets.

Fullerton Park, sadly, as a venue failed to survive World War Two, although Nottingham survived as a greyhound venue until 1970.

I have no personal experience of Fullerton Park, but I did visit Nottingham White City shortly before its closure, in the company of former rider Fred Strecker, who with his one-time riding partner George Dykes ran a car-breaking yard next to the stadium.

The most striking thing about Nottingham on a first visit was the stadium's resemblance to Sheffield's Owlerton arena. A substantial main grandstand, by the time of my visit with most of the accommodation behind plate glass, covered terracing on both the first and fourth bends (in Nottingham's case with some seating), and a large totalisator board on the approach to the back straight.

The length of the White City track at 380 yards was more or less the same as Owlerton today.

During the reconstruction the greyhound and speedway tracks were sited at a higher level than the original circuits. This meant that there was a substantial slope from the inner edge of the speedway track down to the level of the centre green.

Nottingham White City from the air, showing the track's proximity to the River Trent. Ferry services operated to the stadium on speedway nights, from Trent Bridge, upstream of the White City and close to the famous test match cricket ground and the homes of Nottingham Forest and Notts County. The car breaking yard above the third bend was operated by Nottingham speedway riders Fred Strecker and George Dykes. (AC)

There is plenty of anecdotal, and some documentary evidence, to suggest that promoters did approach the White City management, not just immediately after World War Two but at intervals right through to the stadium's closure. The White City management had no desire to see speedway return. The track itself was concreted over and used to parade the dogs on greyhound nights.

The only post-war speedway to take place in Nottingham following World War Two was on a grass track, sanded on the bends, situated at Highfields in the west of the city, off University Boulevard. Belle Vue stars Dent Oliver and Louis Lawson (a Nottinghamshire man) rode here, together with many other league riders of the era.

Speedway in Nottingham was more or less consigned to the past, despite Long Eaton operating for a couple of seasons (1979-80) as Nottingham Outlaws.

Plymouth St Boniface Arena

The argument over whether speedway constitutes more of a spectacle on the big, full-throttle-all the-way-round circuits which formed the majority in days gone by, or on the tighter tracks that predominate today, has raged for decades and will probably never go away.

When postwar speedway hit a then record total of 35 league tracks in 1951, just three venues had a track length of less than 300 yards (275 metres), compared to 13 which exceeded 400 yards (366 metres). New Cross, at 262 yards (240 metres) was the smallest, with Liverpool, at 446 yards (408 metres) the biggest.

Today, 18 of the 28 league tracks which went to the tapes for the 2013 season are 275 metres (300 yards) or less.

Very considerably less, in the case of Plymouth's modern venue, the St Boniface

Plymouth's compact St Boniface Arena is overshadowed by a major road flyover. (BL)

Arena, which at just 216 metres (236 yards) is by some way the smallest track in UK competitive speedway, and considerably smaller than New Cross. It is not, however, the smallest track to ever stage league speedway in Britain. Linlithgow in Scotland competed in the British Conference League in 1999 on a 234 yard (fractionally under 214 metres) circuit.

The present-day Devils boast crowds impressive by modern standards, so their supporters seem to appreciate racing on the tight circuit. Older Plymouth fans, who watched racing at the former Pennycross Stadium, which had a track length of 413 yards when it last staged league speedway in 1969, have no doubt adapted to the more intimate atmosphere of the St Boniface Arena.

Spectator seating at the St Boniface Arena, Plymouth. (BL)

The size of the race track obviously depended to a large degree on the confines of the site, which is tucked under the elevated A38 Devon Expressway at Marsh Mills, on the outskirts of the city (shades of the flyover which dominated Cleveland Park, Middlesbrough in the track's latter years).

Unusually, the owner of the land leased by the speedway promotion and after which the venue is named is St Boniface's Catholic College, is a voluntary aided school for boys and sixth-form girls.

The sport was reintroduced at National League level by Mike Bowden in 2006, after a gap of 36 years, and the new Devils have gone some way towards plugging the gap left by the demise of one-time county rivals Exeter.

A new management team was in place for the 2013 season, headed by former Trelawney, Exeter and Devils' rider Seemond Stephens and Ashley Taylor, a long-term supporter and active member of the track staff at the Arena.

A new two-year lease agreement was reached with the College early in 2013 and in addition to team re-building, the new promotion quickly achieved some impressive improvements to facilities for both riders and spectators.

The St Boniface Arena has seating accommodation on both the home and back straights and standing terracing on both bends.

The St Boniface Arena pictured from the road flyover end, showing the seating on the back straight. (VA)

The venue is another encouraging instance of the investment in speedway by promoters at the newer tracks, where freedom of action is not shackled by the priority given to greyhound racing or other sports activities.

Redcar South Tees Motor Park

Despite the sport's fairly obvious struggle to survive in recent times, a trawl through various website forums is likely to reveal a minority of fans who still believe the main role of a speedway promoter is to sit in the stadium office and count his profits.

Anyone who insists on clinging to a notion that has been out of date for a long time should visit the South Tees Motor Park and have a conversation with Redcar chief Brian Havelock.

Despite his obvious love for the sport, the former rider whose list of tracks spans virtually the whole of the north of England west and east of the Pennines – Sunderland, Berwick, Newcastle, Workington, Middlesbrough and Stoke – has no illusions about the life of a promoter and team manager.

> It's basically all about hard work, all the time. When the public come into the stadium they don't always realise the promoter and the track staff have been at it all day to make sure the fans get their speedway.

My first visit to the South Tees Motor Park coincided with the sort of day the speedway world dreads. Some fine weather, alternating with heavy showers, making track work a real lottery.

It was Ted Flanaghan, who for many years helped keep tracks in trim at Oxford, Leicester, Cradley and elsewhere, who summed up the sport's relationship with water as follows:

> Whatever the weather conditions, it is usually a case of either putting it on or taking it off. Obviously, when the weather is consistently wet or if there is a major downpour before or during the meeting, you have problems. On the other hand, if it is dry then you have to know just how much water to put on to keep the dust down without going too far and ruining the surface. It often seems as if you simply cannot win.

Heavy rain, late in the afternoon, ruined all Brian Havelock's track preparation on the day of my visit. At 7pm, at the time the riders should have been starting to warm up their machines in the pits, he had to take to the track and blade off a mass of sodden shale, effectively preparing the racing surface for the second time in a day.

Steady work by Brian and his staff, while the growing crowd waited patiently, eventually resulted in a surface with which the home and visiting riders and the referee felt comfortable.

Redcar's home on a former steelworks site at the South Tees Motor Park is a classic

No rest for a promoter in Britain's uncertain climate. Heavy rain in the afternoon meant Redcar's Brian Havelock (right) was forced to prepare what virtually amounted to a new track at the last minute for a meeting against Newcastle. (A)

example of how speedway can return to an area after a long absence. The traditional home of the sport on Teesside, Cleveland Park, was sold for development in 1996, with the new venue staging racing for the first time a decade later.

In its heyday, Cleveland Park had substantial spectator facilities. At Redcar, as at most newly-established and purpose-built tracks, simply establishing the race-track and the other essentials such as the safety fence, adequate pits and accommodation for the riders, together with track lighting had to take priority.

Subsequently, the venue has gained a sizeable clubhouse and for the 2013 season fans gained the option of a brand new grandstand, seating around 200 people.

Ideally situated overlooking both the pits and Redcar's famous immensely wide and steeply banked third and fourth bends, the new steel-clad facility in the Bears' colours of red and white, gives a first class view for a very modest additional payment. Brian Havelock explained:

> It has been a case of providing facilities as and when it becomes possible. We've put a lot of money into the new stand – more than we should have spent, probably – but it gives something back to the fans and is proving to be popular.

Gareth Rogers, the man behind Redcar's press and publicity, is particularly well placed to understand just how much progress has been made at Redcar.

> I can especially appreciate the improvements as when I first saw the site in March 2005 it was a rundown quad bike practice track, with a model car circuit below where the pits now are.
>
> Basic though it remains, the club has come a long way since then, with the clubhouse and the stand really improving the comfort and enjoyment of the fans.

The new grandstand at Redcar's South Tees Motor Park is strategically placed for viewing both the racing and the adjacent pits area. (A)

A distant plume of smoke proves that industry is alive and well on Teesside. This view is taken looking towards the home straight from the pits. The new grandstand's position at the end of the fourth bend, where the track slopes dramatically down to the start and finish line, can be clearly seen. (A)

Rye House Hoddesdon

Nothing illustrates the changing face of speedway, particularly in the south of England, as well as the steady rise in status of Rye House.

The homely little venue by the River Lea Navigation in Hertfordshire, in all its various incarnations (seven circuits of various shapes and sizes have been used within the footprint of the arena over seven decades) today stands proud as an established and successful member of the Premier League, and promoter Len Silver has invested heavily in new spectator facilities.

Yet in the days when London's 'Big Five' National League Division One tracks ruled the speedway roost, and indeed for many years after the capital city's grip on the sport was broken, Rye House was essentially a training track, or at best a Sunday afternoon

Fans in the original concrete grandstand at Rye House watch intently as the riders hit the first bend. (IB)

Rye House in an earlier incarnation, in the late 1940s in fact, with Stan Bedford leading Arthur Pilgrim and Reg Fearman (RFC)

outing for fans to enjoy the relaxed atmosphere of racing in the Southern Area League.

The sport's top men did grace Rye House with their presence, but their appearances were generally limited to the occasions when clubs such as Harringay and Wembley hired the circuit for training purposes.

Spectators stand shoulder to shoulder on the terracing along the home straight at Rye House, a testament to the marketing skills of promoter Len Silver and the quality of the overall experience at the Hertfordshire track. (IB)

Rye House survives and thrives due to the persistence of its supporters and the backing of Len Silver. Survival is in the air in that part of Hertfordshire, where a plot was hatched in 1683 by a group of Whigs against the Stuart monarchy.

The plan was for a force of men to be concealed at the spot who would emerge and ambush King Charles II and his brother and heir James, Duke of York as they passed by on their way back to London from Newmarket races. As it was, the races were cancelled due to a major fire in the Cambridgeshire town, and the royal brothers returned to London earlier than expected and lived to reign another day.

Rye House was first used for dirt track racing in 1934, with a cinder surface and a corrugated iron safety fence. Following World War Two the Australian former Test star Dicky Case acquired the circuit, together with the adjacent Rye House public house. Sunday afternoon meetings were organised by Harringay official George Kay.

In 1958 the stadium was re-designed, with a smaller track inside a greyhound circuit installed, and the existing concrete grandstand was added. During the period of the re-construction, a new speedway track was laid where the karting circuit now exists, built and operated by Mike Broadbank.

Rye House continued largely as a training school but when Rayleigh Stadium closed in 1974 Len Silver was able to move the Rockets side into the venue. The track was reduced in length, and banking added, and Rye House at last achieved a place in league speedway, other than the Southern Area League.

The concrete grandstand at Rye House. (IB)

Rye House enjoyed considerable success, latterly under the promotion of Ronnie Russell, until 1993. With no speedway at the circuit for the first time for more than half a century, stock car racing was introduced and a tarmac circuit laid down.

It looked like the end for speedway at the venue, but survival was again on the agenda, thanks to the efforts of a group of fans. A Rockets team was formed to compete in the Conference League and a track share obtained at Mildenhall.

The men behind the project then contacted Len Silver to see if he could help in any way. Initially, Silver sponsored the team through his Silver Ski business, and later purchased the lease from the greyhound promotion.

At first the speedway track had to be laid and lifted each week, but after one season of this arrangement the stock cars were given notice to quite and a new track laid over the tarmac, in a different shape.

Scunthorpe Eddie Wright Raceway

Life in a steel town, which has seen its share of the ups and downs of a contracting industry, is not for the faint-hearted.

Determination and persistence are high on the list of needs if you want to survive, let

A panoramic view of the Eddie Wright raceway at Scunthorpe, the third venue to operate in the North Lincolnshire steel town. Between the car park and the stadium is the training track. (AS/Bullet Images)

alone thrive. The history of speedway in the North Lincolnshire town is an object lesson in overcoming most of the things life can throw at you.

In the 40 plus years since the sport was first staged in the town, Scunthorpe has lost two venues, at Quibell Park, a municipal athletics and cycle arena, and a purpose-built venue at Ashby Ville.

It looks like third time lucky however, with the latest home of speedway, The Eddie Wright Raceway, bidding fair to be a huge success. In 2008, used car dealership Eddie Wright entered into a 29-year sponsorship deal with Scunthorpe Scorpions to rename the track.

The sport had returned to the town after a twenty-year absence in 2005, initially in the Conference League, with the first meeting watched by 1,500 people in arctic conditions. Relief for spectators was soon achieved, with two stands built on the home straight.

After great success in the Conference League, winning every available honour, Scunthorpe were accepted into the second tier Premier League in 2008.

The Scorpions hit the top in 2012, winning the play-off grand final despite finishing second to Newcastle in the Premier League table.

The club has an excellent reputation for fostering young talent and the 2013 starting line-up included four British riders. The club and the town has a great deal of pride in Scunthorpe-born Tai Woffinden, who in May 2013 completed a perfect week by winning both the British Championship and the Czech Republic Grand Prix in Prague.

A close-up of the spectator facilities at the Eddie Wright Raceway. (AS/Bullet Images)

Woffinden grew up in Australia after his parents emigrated there but returned to the UK to start his professional speedway career, at Scunthorpe, in 2006.

Scunthorpe claims to run more speedway events than any track in Britain, with a wide range of amateur meetings, open practices and mini-track sessions providing excellent opportunities for riders to gain track time and develop their skills.

Sheffield Owlerton Stadium

Owlerton, at first sight, appears to be the archetypal dog track. The stadium's capacious car park is dominated by the giant neon sign above the turnstiles, depicting four racing greyhounds in full, garish colour.

It is impossible for any user of the car park to escape the gambling theme, as a large portion of the spaces, even on speedway nights, are reserved for gamblers at the associated casino.

Appearances, in this instance, are deceptive. The stadium was purpose-built for speedway, by a company fronted by pioneer dirt-track riders Spencer 'Smoky' Stratton, Jimmy Hindle and Clem Beckett, who went on to lose his life in the Spanish Civil War.

Despite the obvious modern-day emphasis on greyhound racing, Sheffield's Owlerton Stadium was purpose-built for speedway, in 1929. (A)

A panoramic view of Owlerton Stadium, showing the central grandstand and the covered terraces on bends one, three and four. The row of advertising hoardings in the centre of the shot hide the back straight terrace, now closed for safety reasons. (AC)

The trio acquired the land off the Penistone Road in the steel city and had the stadium ready for racing by the end of March, 1929. Thousands packed into the stadium to see Beckett win the first meeting, raced for the Golden Helmet.

Many more were disappointed when the gates were locked on a full house, including Ernest Palmer and his father. Ernest, who rode in the immediate post-World War Two era for Wombwell, Leicester and Long Eaton, and later managed the Tigers team for legendary promoter Frank Varey, has been a part of speedway in South Yorkshire throughout the track's history, and can still be seen on occasions at Owlerton today, at the age of 93.

After the initial boom, enthusiasm for speedway dipped alarmingly in the north of England in the early 1930s and the management sold out to promoters whose prime aim was to introduce greyhound racing, which made its bow at the stadium in 1932.

Start line action at
Sheffield's Owlerton
Stadium. (AC)

Sheffield's speedway history was chequered indeed for the first thirty years of the track's life, with a five year gap in the mid-1930s, revival in 1946 in the Northern League, and withdrawal from the National League Division Two mid-season in 1950. There was to be no more league racing at Owlerton for a decade.

Since the arrival of Varey and the Provincial League in 1960, speedway has been absent from Owlerton for only two seasons, and Sheffield has for long been regarded as one of the sport's premier venues, with a fast, well-maintained track, excellent racing and facilities for spectators which, by most standards, are top class.

Despite this, the Tigers have operated since 1997 in British speedway's second tier, the Premier League. Yorkshire caution and canniness have prevailed over any ambition for higher status.

In the days before
disasters at football
grounds brought about
stricter safety regulations
at sports arenas,
Owlerton had covered
seating in front of the
main stand, discernible in
this start line shot from
the early 1960s. (AFC)

Owlerton Stadium has certainly seen its ups and downs in recent years. It was inevitable that the disaster that struck at Sheffield Wednesday's Hillsborough ground, just up the road from Owlerton, would have local repercussions as safety became the priority on the sporting agenda.

In September 1989 the local council ordered complete closure of the stadium, which had been home to the Sheffield Eagles Rugby league team in addition to greyhound racing and speedway. Although there were fears that the venue would disappear completely, it was subsequently allowed to re-open, with a drastically reduced capacity.

Owlerton has seen considerable development since its re-opening, but some of its facilities have been lost. Casualties of the emphasis on safety have included the disappearance of the covered seating in front of the glass-fronted grandstand/bar/restaurant, and the closure of the extensive back-straight terrace.

The terrace is still in situ, although the safety barriers have been removed, and remains a forbidden if tantalising area for fans.

The covered terraced areas on both sides of the grandstand (first and fourth bends) are still available, providing spectators with an abundance of sheltered viewing areas that most other tracks can only envy of many other circuits.

Owlerton, with not only excellent facilities but an aura of history conferred by nearly 70 seasons of racing, remains the sort of classic speedway track that provides a superb introduction to newcomers to the sport.

Somerset
The Oak Tree Arena

Somerset Rebels and Buxton Hitmen, the short and the tall of British speedway racing are, to me at least, inextricably linked.

The two clubs, represent the ultimate in the sport's modern ability to establish itself in deeply rural and even highly unlikely geographical situations. The two outfits are in many ways very similar, in other ways completely different.

Beloved of Sky TV, Somerset's Oak Tree Arena has a reputation for a warm welcome and excellent racing. The fans pour into the arena in this shot, with the great bulk of Brent Knoll dominating the rural scene for miles around the Somerset levels. (A)

The short and the tall aspect is simple to explain. The home of the Rebels, the Oak Tree Arena, situated in the tiny village of Edithmead, in the parish of Burnham Without, stands about 10 feet above sea level on the Somerset moors and levels, an area of pasture land drained by an extensive network of dykes, rivers and artificial channels.

The Hi-Edge Raceway, as the name suggests, is at a slightly higher altitude, in fact about 1,790 feet higher!

Somerset raced a challenge match at Buxton in 1999, before the Oak Tree Arena was ready for league speedway. The following year, when the Rebels entered the then

The parade is over and the riders set off on their practice laps, before the start of a local derby between Somerset and Plymouth at the Oak Tree Arena. (A)

The wind can blow chilly over the Somerset levels. These regular fans at the Oak Tree Arena know that it can be wise to gain the shelter of the hedge opposite the first and second turns. (A)

Conference League, the first away fixture was at Hi-Edge – a match I attended.

Supporters of both clubs need to be fairly hardy and determined. The winds whip around the Somerset Levels with just as much force as on Axe Edge. Yet another link is the fact that in each instance, the previous occupants of the terrain occupied today by the Rebels and the Hitmen were sheep.

A virtue shared by the Rebels and the Hitmen is their status as true community clubs, representing the new era in which speedway is promoted not primarily for profit, but is motivated by the sheer passion for the sport possessed by the owners.

The rural, community feel of the Oak Tree Arena is enhanced by the extensive use locals and visitors from farther afield make of the splendid Oak Tree wedding, function and conference centre at the track.

The rural aspect is a positive for the Oak Tree Arena, but that does not mean that Somerset owners Bill and Debbie Hancock, who worked initially with Steve Bishop and are now associated with Gary May, also the Rebels' team manager, have not enjoyed considerable success on track since 2000, rising from the third tier of British speedway to become a power in the Premier League.

The venue has established a powerful reputation in that time, and the quality of racing has made it a favourite with Sky TV cameras.

Debbie Hancock. (CB)

The Hancocks are ambitious, and the current major project is fund-raising for a foam fence.

The Somerset Levels are famous for their sweeping views, and no horizon represents a step too far for Debbie Hancock, as she explained:

> Our aim is eventually to host the bigger events in speedway, such as the Under-21 final and World Cup matches. The big one of course would be to become members of the Elite League, and that is certainly on the agenda for us.
>
> If you think about it, from a geographical point of view, Somerset would be ideal members for the Elite League. The proximity to the motorway makes it easy for both riders and spectators to get here from any part of the country.
>
> Obviously, apart from anything else, we would need a big sponsor. We are constantly working on our facilities and our current project is a polyfoam safety fence, and the supporters are busy helping to raise funds.
>
> We have the big advantage of owning the stadium, which gives us access to the track and facilities for maintenance at any time. We are not at the mercy of greyhound stadium or other managements.
>
> We have come a long way in a short space of time and we believe we can go a lot further.

Looking towards the back straight at Somerset's Oak Tree Arena. The M5 Motorway is just the width of a field behind the fencing at the top of the grass bank. The proximity of the motorway meant that the planners dictated that the track lights at the Arena had to be set at a relatively low height. (A)

Loomer Road, the modern-day home of the Stoke Potters, offers plenty of cover on the home straight, and bar and refreshment facilities above the terrace. (A)

Stoke Loomer Road

Stoke, I should say at the very outset, is one of my lucky speedway tracks. Spectators, just as much as riders, have tracks which seem to be constantly associated with good fortune, especially where the weather is concerned.

Stoke always comes up trumps for me, both weather wise and in the conduct of the meetings. In a climate often more suited to ice racing than speedway, I remember a glorious summer evening when the sun was still beating on the sweltering Loomer Road terraces as the match drew to a close.

My luck held when I decided to attend Stoke's 40th anniversary meeting. A few days earlier my car had been stuck fast in an eight foot Peak District snow drift, and as I drove to Chesterton across the Staffordshire hills there were still great piles of the stuff by the roadside.

Stoke feels like the sort of place where speedway should flourish. It is (just) within the sport's West Midlands heartland, and Potteries crowds in the past have at times been large and enthusiastic.

The cold statistics tell a slightly different story. The Potters have existed for a total of 52 seasons but, as the anniversary meeting confirmed, 40 of those have been recorded since the April 1973 opening of Loomer Road. The club's ancestral home at Sun Street,

Start line activity during Stoke's anniversary meeting staged to celebrate 40 years at Loomer Road. (A)

in Hanley, one of the five (really six) towns immortalised by the locally-born novelist Arnold Bennett, actually had a much more chequered history than the current venue.

The Stoke speedway history began in April 1929, but throughout the late 1920s and 1930s, Sun Street saw only a sparse amount of racing. Riding as Hanley, a team entered the English Dirt-track League in 1929 but withdrew after just one league match had been staged at home.

A side re-named as Stoke entered the National League Division Two for the ill-fated 1939 season. Long before Adolf Hitler caused a premature end to the British speedway season, Stoke had thrown in the towel, with the side's fixtures being taken over by Belle Vue Reserves.

The advent of Division Three in 1947 brought a return to the sport, again as Hanley, and this time the club (which reverted back to Stoke in 1952), survived for seven seasons, winning Division Two in 1949.

The third coming of speedway to the Five Towns came with the creation of the Provincial League in 1960, welcomed by a 10,000 crowd at Sun Street. The stadium closed for re-development at the end of 1963.

Nearly a decade passed before a consortium led by Russ Bragg acquired land on the industrial fringe of Newcastle-under-Lyme. The name game which had dogged speedway in the Potteries throughout its existence persisted, and initially the new side had to operate under the name of Chesterton, the district in which the stadium actually stands, because of objections to the title of Stoke from the management operating Crewe.

When Loomer Road was first constructed, the intention was to build a long track outside the speedway circuit. It is still possible to see where the first and second bends of the long track were intended to be, and this picture shows that the terracing at the venue extends far beyond the point where the first bend curves around from the home straight. (A)

Although the Stoke name was revived in 1974, there have been many management changes at Loomer Road. In 1996, after a single blank season at the venue, the homeless Cradley side rode at the venue for a season under the name of Cradley Heath and Stoke Potters.

In recent years, Stoke has experienced ups and downs, but has managed to survive, albeit dropping down from the Premier League to the National League for the 2011 season.

Loomer Road is an interesting venue, one which has been smartened up considerably by Dave Tattum and his team. Viewing from the partly-covered terraces is good and trackside parking is available on the back straight and third and fourth bends.

When originally constructed, the plan was for the speedway track to sit inside a much larger long-track circuit. To this day, the terracing on the home straight stretches way past the first turn of the speedway track and the banking beyond what would have been the first two bends of the long-track is also clearly visible.

A large and expectant crowd at Swindon's Abbey Stadium waits for the tapes to go up, with the resurgent Robins chasing the Elite League title in 2012. (AC)

Swindon Abbey Stadium

There are towns and cities in England where speedway is neglected and unloved by the powers that be.

There are places where, when the future looks bleak, councillors vow they will go to the stake rather than see their local stadium fall to the developer's bulldozers. But when push comes to shove, the same councillors sit on their hands and do nothing at all.

The all-too-common tales of apathy, and sometimes downright hostility to the shale sport, make people in Swindon scratch their heads in bewilderment.

For the Wiltshire town loves its speedway. Not just the hardcore fans of the Robins, but the place as a whole.

Unusually for what is primarily a greyhound stadium, Swindon retains a covered stand on the back straight at Blunsdon. (A)

In fact, there is a strong argument that without the powerful support of the local authority Swindon fans might have been mourning the loss of the sport, rather than celebrating a famous 2012 victory over Poole in the two-legged Elite League play-off final.

The greyhound company which owns Swindon's Abbey Stadium, situated on the outskirts of the town at Blunsdon, working with financial backers, applied for planning consent to redevelop the Abbey Stadium.

The plans envisage a new stadium to the side of the present circuit, occupying what is currently the main car parking area. The land vacated under the redevelopment would be used for new housing and business units.

As Robins owner Gary Patchett puts it, the new fourth bend of the speedway track would just about clip the location of the current first bend.

The major problem with the plans for Patchett and his team was the fact that, under the plans as originally submitted, there would have been no fourth bend. In fact the redevelopment plans did not include a new speedway track at all.

The threat to speedway caused a local outcry, and Swindon being Swindon, the outraged supporters found they had an ally in the local authority. Gary Patchett explained:

> The council made it clear that in their view, speedway was essential to Swindon. As it was, the plans were put on the back burner because of the recession, but without the council support Swindon speedway could have been dead by now.

The local authority eventually did grant the stadium owners planning permission, but only with the proviso that the redevelopment includes a speedway track. At the time of writing, Patchett and his co-promoter Alun Rossiter believed building work could begin later in 2013.

Swindon have raced at Blunsdon every year since the club was created by businessman Bert Hearse in 1949. The loyalty of the local fans meant the Robins

A threatening sky and the fact that the covers have not been placed on the dog track at Swindon's Abbey Stadium (although the tyres are in place ready to hold down the tarpulins) says it all — match postponed. The crowds will not throng the grandstand area and the home straight standing areas on this occasion. (A)

survived the downturn of the early and mid-1950s, and won the National League Division Two championship in 1956.

When the withdrawal of Wembley forced the remaining 11 teams to form one single division National League for 1957, Swindon surprised the speedway world by winning the title, and the Robins were British League Champions in 1967. More than forty years were then to elapse before the 2012 Elite League success.

The Abbey Stadium has been home to many star names, from Ken Middleditch, George White, Bob Roger and Mike Broadbank, through multi-World Champion Barry Briggs, local boys Bob Kilby and Martin Ashby, Phil Crump, father of World Champion Jason, right through to the present-day heroes of the Elite League-winning side.

Over the years, despite the World Champions and Grand Prix superstars, few men have proved as popular at Blunsdon as present-day co-promoter and team-manager Alun Rossiter

The Swindon-born Rossiter represents the loyalty and pride in the Wiltshire town that has carried the Robins through sixty-four years of continuous speedway.

With the backing of the local council and the community as a whole, the Robins are looking forward to many more years of speedway at Blunsdon.

Tamworth The Stadium, Fazeley

Tamworth's contribution to speedway history was limited to just four seasons, at the height of the sport's post-war boom. The Staffordshire track never ranked among the aristocrats of the sport, but its idiosyncrasies have ensured it an enduring place in speedway folklore.

Although the teams that raced at the Fazeley stadium may not have been out of the top drawer, the setting for speedway was rooted in a unique and undeniably blue-blooded setting.

Pre-war rider and multi-track promoter Arthur Westwood, a contender for the title of speedway's most loveable rogue, was no great respecter of tradition.

When he made a return to the sport in 1947, he chose a site which had formed part of the ancient deer park of Drayton Manor, the home of former Tory Prime Minister Robert Peel, founder of a police force still widely known, in his honour, as 'bobbies'.

Tamworth Stadium's Sports Club and covered standing area, pictured in the years after speedway had vanished from the Fazeley arena. Greyhound racing was a late addition to a venue purpose-built for speedway. At that time an effort was made to make the hare actually look like a long-eared creature rather than just a lump of foam rubber. (TH/JH)

Whether Arthur, who had one or two brushes with the law himself when attempting to promote speedway in France and Belgium, saw the irony of the Peel connection, we will never know.

Legend has it that the site taken up for the stadium had also been used for cricket, once honoured with an appearance by the formidable Dr W. G. Grace (who appears to have played on more grounds than most people in his era had hot dinners).

Arthur built on a speedway tradition established in the 1930s when non-league racing took place at two venues in Mile Oak, another suburb of Tamworth, when he launched the Hounds into the new Division Three of the National League. At any track where he was in charge – and his pre-World War Two record had at one stage included Nottingham, Leeds, Sheffield and Birmingham Hall Green all at the same time – there was never a dull moment.

The speedway angle in this shot of Tamworth Stadium concerns the small bungalow behind turns one and two. When former Birmingham rider Phil 'Tiger' Hart managed Tamworth on behalf of Brummies boss Les Marshall, he and his family, including future rider John, actually lived within the stadium. (TH/JH)

Tamworth's opening meeting was given a lively send-off by the presence of top comedian, speedway fan and rumoured investor George Formby, then one of Britain's greatest stars of stage and screen.

Australian veteran Steve Langton and Cyril Page, who was to ride for most of the Midlands tracks in the post-war era, were the initial mainstays of the Tamworth team and the Hounds soon established a reputation for developing talent.

After Birmingham chief Les Marshall took over at Fazeley, a long list of riders from Tamworth found their way into the Birmingham Brummies team over the years (often also including a spell at Cradley Heath), including Australian Arthur Payne, Eric Boothroyd, Harry Bastable, Lionel Watling, Dick Tolley, and Ivor Davies.

Tamworth also provided an important milestone in the career of one of the most exciting riders of speedway's post-World War Two golden era, the Australian blonde bombshell Graham Warren.

Warren, without a contract when he arrived in Britain in 1948, was given a trial at Birmingham after failing to persuade West Ham of his talent. Brummies promoter Les Marshall signed him for his other interest, Division Three side Cradley Heath.

A sad picture of desolation at Tamworth in the early 1960s. Speedway had a short existence at Fazeley, stock car racing came to what seemed like a premature end, and the investment in greyhound racing facilities such as the substantial totalisator board in this shot failed to pay a lasting dividend. (TH/JH)

Graham Warren rode just one match for the Heathens, at Tamworth, scoring eleven points from his four rides and beating the track record set by fellow countryman Payne. That was the sum total of his Cradley career, as stardom beckoned with the Brummies.

The initial enthusiasm of the Tamworth crowd, drawn from a wide area as far north as the mining areas of South Derbyshire, gradually waned. Although the Hounds generally did well on the track, finishing third in Division Three in 1949, Westwood was losing money and pulled out of Tamworth in favour of continental adventures.

The track's close links to Birmingham ensured survival for one more season. Fazeley was promoted in 1950 by Les Marshall, with former Perry Barr star Phil 'Tiger' Hart as manager, and with the team name changed to the Tammies.

Hart moved his family to Tamworth as part of the deal, actually living in a bungalow within the stadium grounds – the speedway equivalent of the flat above the shop.

Phil's son John, who was to enjoy a long career with Cradley, Sheffield, Leicester and Birmingham, recalled how on the evenings when the stadium was staging greyhound racing, he and his sister Barbara would climb out of a window and make their way underneath the wooden terracing of the grandstand in search of extra pocket money.

Their purpose was to pick up the loose change that the punters, in either triumph or desperation, would drop through the slats of the terracing.

Fazeley Stadium, despite claims of covered accommodation for 5,000, was fairly basic, with a clubroom, and a small stand with terracing constructed from cinders and old railway sleepers in front. The most imposing building was the sizeable totalisator board for greyhound racing.

The dogs continued to race at Fazeley into the 1960s and the speedway track was used by stock cars well into that decade. Today, the stadium has been obliterated by housing.

Weymouth Radipole Lane

John Pilblad is a natural candidate for the title of speedway's patron saint of lost causes. Like many saints, John also endured martyrdom at the hands of the sport's controlling bodies.

A man who reached the very top in a demanding profession, as the BBC's top outside broadcast cameraman, he never quite managed to clamber over the many and varied obstacles laid down in his path by the Control Board and, it has to be said, many of his fellow promoters.

Speedway, in its prosperous years, was unashamedly a business and at times a cut-throat one. Throughout the mid to late 1950s, at the post war low point of the sport's fortunes, and when riders were being forced out of the game through lack of bookings and the consequent lack of income, would-be promoters willing to risk their capital in re-opening closed tracks were given little encouragement.

Pilblad was first and foremost a fan, whose love for the game was nurtured at Blackbird Road in his home town of Leicester. John later served in the RAF and then in 1954 found himself in London, where he gravitated to the terraces at Wimbledon's Plough Lane.

When he heard on the grapevine that there was an opening for someone to run speedway again at Aldershot's Tongham Stadium, John jumped in

The original Radipole Lane Stadium at Weymouth, in the condition that new promoter John Pilblad discovered when he set out to restore speedway to the Dorset seaside resort. (JP)

feet first and, courtesy of his new found status as the promoter of a Southern Area League team, was in at the birth of the Provincial League.

With the encouragement of Mike Parker, John entered the Shots for the new competition, but the Control Board vetoed the application, together with that of fellow Southern Area Leaguers Eastbourne.

John now turned his attention to Weymouth, without speedway since a short-lived attempt to run National League Division Two racing in 1955. With a band of helpers, he worked tirelessly to bring the virtually derelict track and stadium at Radipole Lane up to scratch.

Again, the result was to be heartbreak. An application to join the expanding Provincial League for 1961 was turned down, without even the consolation of an open licence. The Control Board believed a seaside track with its crowd potential restricted to the peak holiday season was not suitable for league racing.

Pilblad, despite his blossoming professional career with the BBC was persistent. An open licence was granted for 1962 and although rain wrecked the opening night for the new Weymouth Royals, speedway was back in the resort, with John at the helm.

The Royals made it through 1963 and 1964, although Provincial League promoters became increasingly reluctant to loan out their young riders to non-league circuits. Weymouth was always something of a Cinderella venue, and although the track was a founder member of British League Division Two in 1968, the venture only lasted a season.

The Dorset club's best spell in speedway lasted from 1974 through to 1984, as members of BL Division Two and subsequently the National League. In early 1985, with re-development of the site envisaged – a new stadium for Weymouth Football Club was eventually built on the site – the licence was switched to Poole.

Both speedway in Weymouth and John Pilblad's career as a promoter were to enjoy a further lease of life.

John Pilblad initially enjoyed a certain amount of success at Weymouth, This start line shot features a challenge match against Exeter in the early 1960s. (JP)

Arch-enthusiast John Pilblad, a top BBC Outside Broadcast cameraman in his highly-successful professional life, was never afraid to roll up his sleeves to further his speedway promotional ambitions. Radipole Lane at Weymouth was in a poor state of repair, so Pilblad (third from left holding the wire) set to with other enthusiasts to erect fencing and other facilities. (JP)

Weymouth re-opened at a new venue, the Wessex Stadium, next to the former site, in 2003, racing initially in the third tier Conference League (winning the title in 2008) and then, until the end of the 2010 season, in the National League.

John Pilblad's final fling with speedway was at Ipswich, which he had re-opened in 1964 for matches in an SAL-type competition called the Metropolitan League, for which the fixtures were never completed. He ran some open meetings in 1965 but although crowds were good for the revival, clashes with other promoters and broken promises made life virtually impossible. A final straw came when Wimbledon pulled out of an agreement to send a side to Foxhall Heath. John explained:

During all the years I was promoting speedway, I had countless clashes with the Control Board and with some individual promoters. I was not out to make money, just to break even and provide fans at some of the lesser tracks with speedway. I always paid the appropriate rates and made sure the riders were fully insured, but although some promoters, particularly Len Silver, were helpful, others were obstructive.

Chapter Seven

MULTI-PURPOSE ARENAS
– Penny Farthings to Prize Bulls

Birmingham The Alexander Stadium   **Isle of Wight** Smallbrook Stadium

Lakeside Arena Essex   **Long Eaton** Station Road

Peterborough The East of England Showground

Many, perhaps most of the stadia which have featured in earlier chapters, fall into the category of multi-purpose arenas.

The original Wembley Stadium, built for the British Empire Exhibition, was subsequently the setting for events of all kinds, from fervent religious rallies to the regular greyhound meetings which were initially condemned as wicked by the established church.

Until the recent arrival of tracks used almost exclusively for speedway, most venues where the sport was (or still is) staged were also home to at least

one regular activity, whether the dogs, football, rugby, or athletics. The majority have over the years also staged many occasional or one-off events, such as stunt shows and carnivals, while stadium car parks often provided a stopping place for travelling fun fairs and circuses.

The venues featured in this chapter stand out for various reasons, and particularly for their origins. Long Eaton's always unfashionable Station Road venue, over more than a century of use as a base for leisure activities, played host to a variety of sports probably unmatched by any other UK venue.

Lakeside's home at the Arena Essex Raceway is notable for being one of the very few venues purpose-built for stock car racing, and where the four-wheeled sport, which has usually over the years moved in cuckoo-fashion at existing speedway tracks, has the longer history.

The speed thrill at the Recreation Ground in Long Eaton in 1888 was cycling, with world endurance records set on the circuit which was later transformed into a greyhound and speedway stadium. The distinctive building behind the riders was incorporated into the Pavilion Hotel, behind the grandstand at Station Road, and a familiar sight for home and away speedway fans in later days. (LEPL)

The grandstand at the East of England Showground, which today is as familiar with racing motorbikes as it is with prize bulls and showjumping, holds 2,300 spectators. (A)

Above right: If only speedway could enjoy weather conditions of this kind every week! Lakeside's home at the Arena Essex Raceway, a circuit created for stock car racing and now home to a variety of motor sport, including, of course, speedway, has excellent bar and refreshment facilities. (BL)

Explaining the convoluted history of the arena which for much of its lifespan existed as the original Alexander Sports Stadium at Perry Barr, Birmingham, is a daunting task. One undisputed fact is that the site, now happily hosting speedway again, was constructed for athletics and cycling.

Peterborough Panthers' home at The East of England Showground, as the name suggests, had a primarily agricultural role. Speedway has been established in the main show ring at Alwalton for forty-three years and its long history inevitably begs the question as to why the sport has not sought similar venues elsewhere.

Rural settings usually well-removed from nearby housing development, extensive car parking and other facilities, and spectator accommodation often well above the minimum needed for staging speedway are among the advantages to be found at the permanent showcases for agricultural excellence.

Australian agricultural showgrounds, with Johnnie Hoskins' venture at West Maitland to the fore, were in at the birth of speedway racing as we know it today.

Speedway-style grass track racing in the main arena of a British agricultural show was at one time a popular way to bring the event to a spectacular close, at venues as far afield as the Welsh National's headquarters at Builth Wells and the Duke of Hamilton's showground in Scotland, where meetings were arranged by Ian Hoskins.

In recent years the sport was staged at the United Counties Showground near Carmarthen in West Wales, where photographs show the adjacency of typical agricultural buildings to the actual racetrack.

Birmingham The Alexander Sports Stadium

Speedway's older venues are chock full of memories. At Brandon, Owlerton, Brough Park, Monmore Green and the Abbey Stadium, the spirits of long gone riders mingle with vanished armies of terrace fans.

Prosperity: A composite picture of the Alexander Sports Stadium, Perry Barr, Birmingham, during the immediate post-World War Two era, after the construction of terracing all around the arena allowed a big increase in spectator capacity and led to the staging of test matches at the venue. (BB)

The feeling of the past being only a blink of the eye away from the present is perhaps nowhere stronger than at Perry Barr, Birmingham. The present-day Greyhound Stadium, with its brand spanking new glass-fronted grandstand, is quite literally superimposed upon the footprint of the previous occupier of the site, the original Alexander Sports Stadium – the classic home of speedway's Brummies.

Today's spectators at Perry Barr are confined to restricted areas of what is a typically modern dog track, designed for the comfort of a relatively small number of greyhound punters, many of whom are primarily attracted by a party atmosphere.

Although the speedway management at Perry Barr has had to grapple with the issue of how to make watching speedway relatively comfortable (see page 51), the problem is a minor one compared to the challenge facing immediate post-war promoter Les Marshall.

The Alexander Sports Stadium, constructed for the Birchfield Harriers, perhaps Britain's premier athletics club, had only a single grandstand, of traditional construction and with a limited capacity.

This meagre facility had sufficed for the mixed programme of athletics, cycle racing and, later on show-jumping, which entitled the stadium to the status of a multi-purpose arena.

Enthusiasm for speedway in the 1940s gripped England's second city and Marshall somehow coaxed the authorities into giving consent for building work. He found the cash and materials to terrace the entire stadium, giving a capacity in the region of 40,000, sufficient to stage National League Division One speedway and test matches.

Les Marshall's investment is one of several instances that disapproves the popular belief that British promoters failed to invest in facilities during the sport's golden age. It was also Marshall who installed the lighting system at the Alexander Stadium, facilitating Britain's first floodlit athletic meeting and also show jumping under lights.

The hard work and investment in erecting the terracing eventually came to nothing. Birmingham withdrew from the National League in 1957 (there was a revival on an open licence in 1960 promoted by Phil 'Tiger' Hart and Doug Ellis, at one time chairman of Aston Villa, but the athletics club proved to be difficult landlords.

Ruin: The grandstand at the Alexander Sports Stadium stands isolated, with everything else demolished, after the owners, Birchfield Harriers Athletic Club, abandoned the site for a new arena not far away in Perry Barr. The present Perry Barr Greyhound Stadium (the second venue to carry that name) now stands on the site pictured. The one constant presence is the row of houses in the background.

The Alexander Sports Stadium grandstand in its speedway heyday in the 1950s, with the riders parading for a World Championship qualifier. Visible are, l-r Tommy Miller (Glasgow Tigers), Maury Dunn (Harringay), Danny Forsberg (Birmingham), signing an autograph close to the fence, Graham Warren of Birmingham, and Stig Pramberg of Vargarna (Sweden). Alan Hunt and Ron Mountford, both of Birmingham, can be seen towards the right of the picture. (GB)

Birchfield Harriers then moved to a new arena of the same name just down the road, and their original home was derelict for some time, with the terracing bulldozed. The transfer of athletics elsewhere at least opened the door for the new greyhound venue and, eventually for a speedway revival.

One link between the past and the present is a bas relief of the Birchwood Harriers coat of arms, incorporated into the present-day Perry Barr Greyhound Stadium grandstand façade.

Smallbrook Stadium, Ryde, Isle of Wight, is one of speedway's less glamorous venues, but has the distinction of being Britain's only offshore club and home to the sport's biggest track. (BL)

Isle of Wight Smallbrook Stadium, Ryde

The legendary Shadows guitarist Jet Harris made his home on the Isle of Wight during his latter years. He made a point of emphasising to his concert audiences that The Solent, which separates the island from the English mainland, was the most expensive stretch of water in the world to cross by ferry.

Harris would then bring the house down by claiming that this was never a problem during his years touring with Cliff Richard, who was able to walk on water.

The Isle of Wight Islanders speedway team, the only side in British speedway history to require away teams and supporters (and probably some of its own fans) to travel by sea or air to matches, has its own solution to crossing the water.

The team's main sponsor at the time of writing was Wightlink Ferries, and the company offered special deals for trips from Portsmouth, including a catamaran crossing of The Solent, a taxi ride from Ryde Pier head to Smallbrook Stadium, and admission to the speedway.

It is a deal unique in the speedway world, which before the birth of Isle of Wight Speedway in 1996 had counted a much less ambitious 1930s amphibious journey along

Smallbrook was once home to the now defunct Ryde Sports FC. The centre green, as seen in this photograph, would no longer be considered suitable for senior non-league football. The stadium also has the facilities for indoor activities in the large sports hall behind the home straight grandstand. (BL)

the River Trent in Nottingham, taking fans from Trent Bridge, close to the famous test cricket ground, on a short cruise due east to the White City Stadium as its only form of waterborne transport.

Speedway first came to the island in May 1996, and in 1997 island fans got their first taste of league racing when the ill-fated Skegness Braves side completed their Premier League fixtures at Smallbrook Stadium, riding as the Isle of Wight.

The Islanders enjoyed considerable success at Premier League Level, winning the Young Shield twice and the knock-out Cup once, together with double victories in the Pairs Championship and a single triumph in the Four Team Tournament.

Adam Shields brought individual success to the club when he won the 2002 Premier League Riders Championship and five years later the Premier League Pairs and Four Team Tournament sides both included 2012 World Champion Chris Holder, who made his British debut for the Isle of Wight in 2006.

The Islanders dropped down from the Premier League to the third-tier National League for the 2009 season.

Smallbrook Stadium opened in April 1971 and initially functioned as an athletics track with a cinder surface. A football pitch in the centre was used by Ryde Sports FC, which moved from its former ground when Smallbrook opened.

The stadium's use for athletics came to an end in 1993, when a synthetic track opened elsewhere on the island, and the circuit was disused until converted into a speedway circuit. Ryde Sports, a club with a history dating back to 1888, folded in 1997. The Isle of Wight Hockey Club also plays its home matches at the stadium.

Smallbrook has a 440-seat covered stand, typical of those to be found at non-league football grounds throughout the country, grass banking on the first bend, and a premier lounge bar on the second bend, as part of the indoor facilities of the stadium.

One distinction Smallbrook holds is that of being by some distance the biggest track in British speedway's three divisions, at 385 metres (420 yards).

Lakeside Arena Essex Raceway

There are several good reasons why the Arena Essex Raceway qualifies for inclusion in a chapter devoted to speedway's quirkier venues.

The location, for one thing, makes it stand out from the crowd. Speedway tracks can be found in all sorts of places, rubbing shoulders with inner-city industrial regions (Sheffield), genteel leafy suburbs (Coventry) and the windswept grandeur of the Derbyshire hills (Buxton).

The surroundings of Arena Essex are neither industrially grim, neatly suburban, nor rurally attractive, but they accurately reflect life in the 21st century. The venue sits in the midst of a bewildering maze of motorway and arterial road intersections, huge traffic roundabouts, service areas, and one of Europe's largest shopping malls.

The substantial home straight covered area at the Arena Essex Raceway, home base for the Lakeside speedway club. (BL)

Twist number two for Arena Essex is that it is one of the very few stadiums originally constructed for stock car racing. In most instances the stox arrived long after the bikes were already established.

The third unusual element is that the early speedway meetings at the track were run without the benefit of a safety fence.

The 290-yard (265 metre) speedway circuit sits inside a near quarter mile asphalt track designed for the various types of short circuit car racing which take place at the venue. For some time the fact that this offered a run-off for the bikes and their riders in case of need was considered sufficient.

Arena Essex and its speedway team (originally named after the circuit and now re-christened Lakeside) is the nearest thing to a speedway track possessed by a city (London) which once dominated the sport almost entirely.

With the failure of the Wimbledon revival in the early days of the new millennium, the capital is a speedway desert. Londoners looking for a night at speedway (who once had a choice of five Division One tracks racing on each week night), now have Arena Essex. The stadium is 20.4 miles from Charing Cross, the point in London from which distances are traditionally measured.

Perhaps more to the point, Arena Essex is roughly 14 miles from the site of West Ham's former Custom House Stadium.

Given the number of East Enders who have moved north east into the county of Essex, including no doubt many former West Ham fans, it comes as no surprise that the Lakeside team are the Hammers, with their race suits carrying the famous crossed hammers symbol of their illustrious predecessor at Custom House.

Some of the original Hammers fan base may survive, but it would be idle to pretend that the glamour of Custom House is still there.

Just as the surroundings of Arena Essex represent life as it is in the second decade of the new millennium, the venue is typical of present-day speedway stadia. The track was the brain-child of stock car driver and promoter Charles 'Chick' Woodruffe, who had it built on a site which previously acted as an overflow for a cement works.

Arena Essex certainly doesn't lack essential creature comforts. There is a substantial covered standing area, also housing race control, on the home straight and The Raceway Tavern, overlooking the first bend, is a well-appointed bar and lounge area with a balcony.

A close-up view of the covered area at Arena Essex, with the referee's box slung below the roof girders and a TV/Video filming point up above. Referees and other officials often need a head for heights when scaling ladders to their duty stations. (BL)

The banking which surrounds the car and speedway tracks has plenty of spectator potential. If the arena had concrete terracing, it would probably have the largest capacity of any current speedway track.

The memorial meeting for the Lakeside rider Lee Richardson, tragically killed in Poland at the start of the 2012 season, reportedly attracted a crowd of some 6,000, with room to spare.

Long Eaton Station Road Stadium

High-speed racing on two wheels, with riders in close contact, was a major attraction for thrill-seeking crowds at Station Road, Long Eaton, in September 1888.

Obviously, the attraction was not motorcycle speedway, still four decades away from its British debut. What the Long Eaton fans witnessed in 1888 was pedal power in action, with star cyclists such as the American champion Stillman G. Whittaker setting world records in against-the-clock and other events, riding machines which in some respects resembled penny farthings but which were known as highwheel racers.

Whittaker, who rode all over the world at top-class velodromes nevertheless rated Long Eaton as his favourite British circuit.

Houses now occupy the site of Long Eaton Stadium, originally opened in 1884 as the Recreation Ground, which over its active life of more than 110 years was home at various times to a probably unprecedented variety of both amateur and professional sports.

Long Eaton Stadium under construction in what appears to be a wet January, 1928. The site is now covered by houses, but the high level railway line visible in the background remains in use. The grandstands on the fourth bend were built to a pattern once familiar at greyhound/speedway stadia. (LEPL)

Another shot at Station Road, Long Eaton, shows the main stand under construction, together with the stands on the fourth bend. The Pavilion Hotel, now also disappeared, is behind the embryo main stand. (LEPL)

This aerial view of Long Eaton, taken before the speedway track was installed in 1929, shows the seven separate grandstands initially provided for the stadium. All except the main stand (which was damaged and later rebuilt) burnt to the ground during a fire in 1948. (AC)

Although remembered mainly as the home of speedway and greyhound racing, and as one of the original 1954 stock car racing circuits, the 13-acre site at Station Road merits its place in a section devoted to multi-activity venues because of the amazing diversity of sporting activity it hosted.

The Recreation Ground staged first-class cricket, with Derbyshire meeting Lancashire in the County Championship in 1887, and was one of the grounds used by Long Eaton Rangers Football Club, who beat today's Premiership giants West Bromwich Albion and played in the Football Alliance, the 19th century equivalent of today's Championship, against the likes of Sheffield Wednesday, Nottingham Forest and Newton Heath (later Manchester United).

The venue was converted into a greyhound stadium in 1928, with spectator accommodation provided in seven grandstands. Speedway, which first featured in 1929, continued with gaps until the venue finally closed at the end of the 1997 season.

In the 1950s and 1960s the stadium saw more cycling and football, including FA Cup matches, midget car racing, horse trotting, and professional boxing, together with stock car racing, banger racing, hot rods and stunt shows.

For all too brief a period, superstar Ove Fundin wore the Long Eaton colours in 1966. With the pits and the fourth bend in the background, the crowd swelled by his presence, Fundin parades at Station Road. (JS)

Parts of the original pavilion, built in the 1880s, could still be seen right up to the end of the stadium's existence, built in to the fabric of the adjacent Pavilion Hotel. The eagle-eyed could also detect the existence of charred timbers from the disastrous fire in 1948 which killed many of the greyhounds kennelled at the stadium and destroyed virtually all of the grandstand accommodation.

Long Eaton was never one of sport's glamour venues, but until its last days, remained an integral and much-loved part of the life of a small industrial town.

The local council, which at first declared that it would fight to the end to retain a sporting role for the site, eventually gave way to the tide of housing.

Peterborough The East of England Showground

The huge grandstand that dominates the main ring at the East of England Showground, situated conveniently just off the A1, the famous Great North Road, is an amenity virtually unsurpassed in British speedway.

The facility offers a high level of shelter and comfort on even the coldest and dampest of speedway nights, and gives a superb view of racing on one of Britain's fastest and most spectacular tracks.

With the stalls behind the grandstand providing some of the best food at any British speedway venue (it seems fitting, giving the agricultural nature of the venue), and a well-appointed bar on the first turn, a night at Alwalton can be one of British speedway's most rewarding experiences.

Two questions present themselves. Why is Peterborough the only club currently operating on an agricultural showground? And are there any drawbacks to a venue that really does seem to offer both management and fans the perfect setting for speedway racing?

Panthers co-promoter Rick Frost acknowledges the fact that many people would find it unusual, given the level of facilities present at many of the country's leading show grounds and the usual distance from residential areas, that Peterborough is currently the only speedway club taking advantage.

Currently is the operative word, with talk of a new track on the show ground at Norwich and the possibility that Edinburgh might move to a similar venue.

"There is no doubt that the facilities are excellent here," Rick said. "The grandstand alone holds 2,300 people, so for most meetings, all of our fans can sit in comfort and enjoy the wonderful view of the racing.

"We can also accommodate at least the same number of cars, making the Showground an ideal venue for big meetings.

"The downside is that such excellent facilities are heavily in demand. The

Peterborough, like Arena Essex, has a well-used refreshment and bar facility on the first bend, situated between the grandstand and the pits. (A)

Showground is well used, and the big difficulty we face, if we have postponements, is fitting in dates for additional meetings."

The current Peterborough promotion is acknowledged throughout the sport as being highly ambitious. Their level of commitment and the highly positive speedway experience a night at the Showground offers will surely reap its deserved reward and bring the good times back to Alwalton.

Chapter Eight
THE FUTURE...?
– Belle Vue's Ambition

B ELLE VUE'S National Speedway Stadium project could transform the future of British speedway. Fans not just in the north west but across the whole of the UK are holding their breath, willing the success of a project which has the potential to raise the profile of the sport nationwide.

The proposed National Speedway Stadium in the Gorton district of Manchester, destined for a site next to the existing home of Belle Vue Aces, the Kirkmanshulme Lane Greyhound Stadium, is part of a project to transform East Manchester into a Mecca for the sporting community.

An artists' impression giving an overall view of the proposed National Speedway Stadium in Gorton, Manchester, which will be built on land adjacent to the present Belle Vue Greyhound Stadium at Kirkmanshulme Lane. (BVS/RF)

The design for the grandstand at the proposed National Speedway Stadium, where Belle Vue hope to be in track action in the near future. (BVS/RF)

The main entrance to the proposed National Speedway Stadium, Belle Vue. (BVS/RF)

Manchester City Council in April 2013 gave the go-ahead for the Belle Vue Sports Village, which will include a custom-built new stadium for the Belle Vue Aces. At the time of writing the project was due to go forward to the planning permission stage, with the Aces targeting an opening date of March 2014.

David Gordon, Belle Vue speedway's chief executive officer, said:

> The go ahead for the project from the city council marked a red letter day in the long history of Belle Vue speedway. It marks the start of a new era and gives speedway in Manchester a massive future.

Early discussions on the prospects for a new speedway stadium at Belle Vue soon revealed that David Gordon and the leaders of Manchester City Council shared a common vision.

> The City of Manchester is a globally-renowned sporting centre and as far as both Belle Vue Aces as a speedway club and the City Council were concerned it was clear that only a world-class facility would be acceptable, David emphasised.

> To satisfy the FIM standards for staging the kind of world-class events the City Council wants to see staged at Belle Vue, the new stadium had to be fully compatible.

> Not only will the track have to be of the highest standard, the viewing experience for the spectators will have to be at the same level. Viewing is poor at Kirkmanshulme Lane and that means staying at the current venue is unsustainable.

> Speedway is nothing if it is not a participation event.

The new stadium will also mean that Belle Vue can run on an evening of the club's choice, which will hopefully boost the crowds.

The new stadium will incorporate a multi-purpose astroturf pitch suitable for a multitude of sports including hockey, junior football and lacrosse.

The design for the stadium incorporates a main grandstand to accommodate 2,500 seated spectators, complete with hospitality and executive areas. Fixed terracing around the track will accommodate a further 3,500 spectators, increasing to anywhere between 12,000 to 18,000 spectators in temporary stand seating for major events such as the Speedway World Cup.

Tailpiece

Proud to wear their Eastbourne Eagles colours, Phil Streatfield, who lives near Maidstone in Kent and his dog Tilly, are to be found regularly on the terraces at Arlington Stadium. Phil was formerly a Canterbury supporter. (A)